# Golf

## The Life Story of
## Bob Babbish

# Byron Babbish

Cover Page Photograph: A publicity photograph of Bob Babbish taken by his college, University of Detroit, while he was on the golf team in 1940 and autographed by him.

Title Page Photograph: A blurry close-up shot of a happy Bob Babbish immediately after sinking the winning putt in the 1938 Western Amateur golf tournament.

Published by Aboard & Abroad Productions LLC

www.aboardandabroad.com

2616 Kopson Court, Bloomfield Hills, Michigan 48304

Printed by CreateSpace, an Amazon.com company.

ISBN: 151724899X

ISBN-13: 978-1517248994

## DEDICATION

To my father, Bob Babbish.

# CONTENTS

# ACKNOWLEDGMENTS

Kurt Jung for proofing this book for me. Patricia Higo at the University of Detroit Mercy Library for helping me with information on when Bob attended college there. Also, John King, the Detroit Golf Club Historian, for providing me with information about tournaments held there and for other golf information.

I relied on dozens of newspaper articles from the three Detroit newspapers published from the 1930's through the 1960's as well as articles in newspapers from other cities written about Bob's golf tournaments over the years that his family and later his wife clipped and saved. There was also a box of photographs of golf, family and World War II that survived the years that I used.

I used the book *Majors of Golf* by Morgan G. Brennan for some data about Bob's results in the 1938 and 1940 U.S. Opens and appreciate that it was compiled and made available.

A special acknowledgement to journalist John Walter who wrote so many articles in The Detroit News since the 1930's about Bob. In 1972, John graciously made photocopies of many of them and sent them to Bob.

The University of Detroit Mercy, Bob's alma mater, has created a fund in Bob's honor for their Men's Golf Program. Tax-deductible donations can be made to it at 4001 W. McNichols Rd., Detroit, Michigan 48221-3038. Note that it is in Bob's memory. All of the materials used to write this book have been donated to the University for safekeeping.

# CHAPTER 1
## INTRODUCTION

This book is not only about a great man but also of a great era in America and of a great sport. It is the story of how talent and personality can transcend one's station in life to allow someone to accomplish great things and change one's life. Of how life in America, in this case Detroit, allowed, even encouraged, something like this to happen. It is also the story of how a sport caught America's imagination and became woven into its fabric, allowing poor kids to ride its popularity and propel themselves to the public's attention and fame.

As you have figured out, the great man is Bob Babbish. The era is most of the 20th Century. And the sport is golf.

First and foremost, this is a story of my father, Bob Babbish. But there is no way to separate Bob's story from the stories of America, Detroit and golf. Without the combination of all these this story wouldn't be the same. It would just be the story about a great father and nothing more. Somehow, Bob would say by the grace of God, America and golf allowed him to use his God-given talents as an athlete to take him out of poverty and propel him to the top of the sport of golf leaving a legacy that few have matched. And Bob had a great time doing so, never forgetting his roots as a coal miner's son and never taking his fame for granted.

Always humble and self-effacing, Bob never bragged or tried to impress others with his golfing success. It was often hard to get him to even talk about it. Same with his time as a soldier in World War II, but that was for other, darker reasons. As his son, I knew that I had a famous father and tried to elicit the many stories from him over the years.

My memories of his golf stories were luckily buttressed by a box full of newspaper clippings and photographs about Bob's golf tournaments that I used to weave together the golf story of this book.

My memories of his family stories, of Bob growing up in Pennsylvania and Detroit, didn't have a box of newspaper articles to support them but there are some photographs and I seemed to have remembered these stories better than the golf ones. There is no one around now to confirm or deny or supplement the family stories, as Bob was the last in his family to pass away.

Dad rarely talked to me about World War II so I have little first-hand information on that part of his life. There are a number of photographs he took in his Army position in Europe during World War II that piece together a story on this period of his life that I will try to convey the best I can.

As always seems to be the case, this book was written too late. Bob passed away in 2012 before it was started. I should have written it before then as he was as sharp as a tack until the day he died and would have remembered all the stories and identified all the photographs and filled in all the blanks.

But, lo, better late than never. Maybe the four years after Bob's passing better crystallized his life and story for me, giving me the confidence and desire to write his story. Maybe the lack of facts from the horse's mouth, so to speak, required me to do my research a bit better, probe a bit more, confirm some of the facts and finally read all those newspaper articles that were saved. Hard to tell but I am glad I finally did it. Hopefully you will be too.

# CHAPTER 2
## BEFORE GOLF: 1915 TO 1926

Norbert Robert Babbish was born on June 6, 1915. He was given the Christian name Norbert but there is no indication that he was ever called anything but Robert or Bob. June 6 is the Catholic feast day of Saint Norbert, also known as Norbert of Xanten, who died on that date in 1134. Bob's mother, Anna, about whom you will learn later, named all her children the name of the saint whose feast day was the day of their birth; an old Catholic tradition. It made naming your babies a lot easier than it is now.

On the day of Bob's birth, the news was predominated by World War I, which was just coming up to its first year anniversary and raged for the first three and a half years of Bob's life. In twenty-six years World War II would radically affect Bob's life. And don't forget, in between the two World Wars the Great Depression would land in the middle of Bob's early teenage years, forever forming his way of living. These three worldwide events in many ways were three of the legs that Bob's table of life were supported by, the fourth leg being his strong family life, and how he coped and adapted to these events made him what he was.

Bob lived to be 96 years old, passing away on January 24, 2012. We all thought we would reach 100 as he was doing so well up to his final six months when he had a debilitating stroke that sent him to a nursing home. Though others in his family lived to be 90 plus years of age, he lived the longest, beating his brother John by three years and his mother Anna by four. If you take a minute to recall

3

all that happened in the world between 1915 and 2012, that was Bob's lifetime. From horse-drawn carriages to iPhones, what a remarkable period of time to have lived.

But I am getting a little ahead of myself. To know Bob we have to know his family. Between his mother and father we know most about his mother, Anna.

Anna Marie Krupa was born in 1889 in Posen, Poland. We know nothing about her parents or her life in Poland, but that they were poor; "peasant stock" as Anna would say. She grew up on a farm there and used her farming skills in one way or another her entire life.

When Anna was eleven years old, in 1900, her parents sent her to America alone. She arrived by boat in New York City, going through Ellis Island as all immigrants did back then. It is lost to memory why she was sent to America. Times were not bad in Poland at the time though it was partitioned still between Austria, Russia and Prussia, Anna living in the Austrian area. It was probably to hopefully have a better chance in life than she would have had on the farm there. Also lost to memory was who she was sent to live with in America.

Anna ended up in Helvetia, Pennsylvania, a coal mining town located south of DuBois. There she was married in 1905 at the age of sixteen to a coal miner named Joseph Babiarz. It was an "arranged" wedding so to speak, to have someone take car of Anna in the United States. Anna and Joseph had eight children, two of which died in infancy.

Helvetia was a coal mining town that was started in the 1890's when a six-foot coal seam was found lying just beneath the surface of farm and woodland. The Helvetia Mine located there quickly became one of the largest producers in the region. Schools, stores and churches were built for the miners and their families

Anna Maria Krupa, Bob's mother, on her wedding day in 1905. She was sixteen years old. This is the only childhood photograph known to exist of Anna.

Little is know of Joseph Babiarz, Bob's father. He was born in 1879 so was ten years older than Anna. He was born in Poland too, in some town in the Russian partition. The little that is remembered of Joseph is that he was a hard worker and a big drinker and smoker, typical of coal miners back then.

There are only a few stories of Bob's first seven years growing up in Pennsylvania and they all revolved around life on the farm there. These stories came from Anna, as Bob was too young then to remember much. As they were dirt poor, there are no photographs from this time period.

The Babiarz family (as will be told in a bit, you can probably figure out that "Babbish" was derived from "Babiarz" at a later date) lived in a "company town," one that was owned by the coal mining company that Joseph worked at. As such, you paid rent for your property or house to the coal company, you bought your food and supplies from the store owned by the coal company, you were educated and worshipped at the company school and church and your livelihood was from the coal company. Back then the coal miners had not only a very hard and dangerous job but were treated poorly by the coal company.

The Babiarz family was fortunate to have a small company-owned plot of land in Helvetia that they could farm. They grew some crops to feed the family and had some livestock including chickens and a cow for the same reason. This was all coordinated by Anna, using her farming experience from Poland, and done by the children. Farming there proved to be their way out of poverty and Pennsylvania, as will be seen in a bit. They also took in the occasional boarder, even though there were six kids, as this was an easy way to make some money in the form of rent.

# Certificate of Baptism

✝

### Church of

*St. Anthony*

*Helvetia, Pa.*

### ⟶ This is to Certify ⟵

That _Norbert Babiarz_

Child of _Joseph Babiarz_

and _Anna Krupa_

born in _Helvetia,_ _Pa._
      (CITY)        (STATE)

on the _6th_ day of _June,_ 19 _15_

was

## Baptized

on the _16th_ day of _January_ 19 _16_

According to the Rite of the Roman Catholic Church

by the Rev. _John Lorenc_

the Sponsors being { _Wladislaw Krupa_
                    _Julianna Borowicz_

as appears from the Baptismal Register of this Church.

Dated _April 24, 1951_

_Pastor_

NO. 314 F. J REMEY CO. INC. N.Y

Anna's tales of her visiting the company store to buy food and supplies were always tinged with resentment as the store took advantage of the coal mining families. Prices were outrageously high requiring one to buy on credit and making them more dependent on Joseph having to work in the mines. And the land they rented from the coal mine company wasn't all that good, making it hard to grow food to eat and offering little for the few farm animals they had to feed themselves. Joseph worked 12-hour days, sometimes longer, as there were no unions to negotiate hours of service limits. Many coal miners were injured or killed in the underground mines due to the lack of safety regulations back then.

With the high cost of living on the company land and the low wages Joseph earned mining the company coal, even being able to supply some food for the family from the farm wasn't enough to sustain them. The kids were too young to work for pay yet (though the oldest, John, did work for a short time in the coal mine around 1922). Something had to be done and the ingenious Anna found a way to sustain the family.

There was enacted in 1918 the Wartime Prohibition Act. This led to the passage of the post-war National Prohibition Act, which took effect in January 1920. Both of these made it first illegal to sell then illegal to produce intoxicating liquors (alcohol). One of the problems with Prohibition was that people found ways around it. Anna was one of them.

Thanks to Prohibition, the Babiarz family found a way out of their poverty. By growing corn and sugar beets on their small farm and utilizing the Babiarz boys' ingenuity with mechanical things (another by-product of living on the farm), Anna built and successfully ran Helvetia's first homemade whiskey still and became the city's first "moonshiner." And boy, was Anna's corn whiskey good. She had customers from all over the county coming to the farm to buy her whiskey, including the mayor and other company officials from Helvetia. The whiskey business helped put food on the table and made the Babiarz family less dependent of the coal mine.

By this time around 1920 when Bob was five years old, word was coming from the west that the Promised Land for workers was in Detroit. World War I was over and the new automotive industry based in Detroit had taken off gangbusters. Henry Ford couldn't keep up with demand for his Model T being built at a large factory in Highland Park, Michigan, just north of Detroit, and, in 1917, started building the huge Ford Rouge Complex in nearby Dearborn to build his cars. Ford was building millions of cars a year during this period and needed a lot of people to work for him to build them. And other car companies were forming in Detroit to build cars at this time too. Joseph thought that this would be the savoir of his family and left on his own to establish a home in Detroit. He eventually found a job working for the Detroit Street Railways streetcar operations of the City of Detroit as a tinsmith.

The family's oral history does not elaborate much on all the reasons for Joseph's move to Detroit but it did take two years for his family to follow him there. Bits and pieces of stories relate that he was a hard drinking man and maybe that had something to do with the family staying behind or maybe it prevented him from finding employment in Detroit right away. Regardless, things had gotten better in Helvetia now that the moonshining business was up and running and maybe there was less reason to leave it during that time.

As mentioned, Bob was one of six children. John was

the oldest, born in 1912. For his whole life, John played the father figure to the family including never smoking, drinking or swearing, something that came easily to the other siblings over the years. Then came Frank, born in 1913, Walter in 1914, Bob in 1915 followed by the only girl Rose in 1917 and Chester in 1919. Two additional children were born before John was but died in early infancy, not too unusual an event out on the farm at the time. For some reason Anna remembered one of them the most, Stanley, and mentioned him a number of times to me.

With Joseph gone to Detroit, John the oldest child started working in the coal mines, probably taking his father's job when he left. This didn't last long as John was almost injured in a mining accident one day and Anna refused to let him go back. This was the only story about Helvetia I remember hearing from someone other than Anna as John told it to me. Figuring the moonshining business would sustain them, they stayed on the farm until another event required them to catch up with Joseph in Detroit.

In 1922 the Feds got wind of Anna's illegal moonshining business in Helvetia and Anna got tipped off from a customer that she was about to be raided. Quickly shutting down the still and packing all their belongings, the Babiarz family boarded a train and left Helvetia on June 6, 1922, Bob's seventh birthday, and headed for Detroit.

The train they boarded at Helvetia took them north to Erie, Pennsylvania where they boarded one of the many passenger ships plying the Great Lakes on Lake Erie at the time for Detroit.

The ship ride to Detroit was the earliest story in Bob's life that I remember hearing from him instead of from Anna or John. Bob recalls looking over the side of the large ship from on deck as they were leaving the dock at

Erie and seeing a huge dead fish down below in the water. Bob said that really scared him for some reason, that fish was so big, and he didn't enjoy the cruise to Detroit because of it. I am sure that the circumstances of the hurried departure (fleeing is probably a better word) from the farm to avoid the Feds as well as heading to an unknown place had a lot to do with Bob's bad memories of this event in his life. However, it turned out to be the best thing the Babiarz family ever did.

With all the money Anna made moonshining in Helvetia, the Babiarz family was able to purchase a lot on Moenart Street in a new neighborhood on the northeast side of Detroit located one block south of McNichols Road (Six Mile Road) and build a two-story brick house there, one of the nicest in the neighborhood. It remained their house until Anna moved out of it in the late 1970's, though Chester and later Rose and her husband Joe lived there a few years later. It is no longer standing now, being torn down in the late 1990's as part of the urban renewal process in Detroit that was tearing down abandoned or burned-out homes in blighted neighborhoods.

Moenart Street was in a nice part of Detroit. McNichols Road was a major east/west cross street one block north of their house. A few blocks west on McNichols was Davison Road and there were a lot of stores at that intersection, including a soft ice cream shop that the Babiarz family started and ran for years. Just north a couple of miles it was still all farmland at that time.

The Polish town of Hamtramck was located just a mile or so west of Bob's home on Moenart. Hamtramck was a city that the City of Detroit grew around as it was expanding at this time but never absorbed. You will hear more about Hamtramck later in this book.

The house Bob grew up in was torn down in the 1990's as a result of the demolishing of abandoned homes in blighted neighborhoods in Detroit. Above is a picture of a house still standing as of 2015 on Moenart Street in Detroit that is located three lots down from where Bob's house was. Bob's house was a very similar style to this one with the attic converted into a dormitory to add more living space to it. In the later years she lived there, Bob's mother Anna used to rent out the upstairs or one of the adult kids would use it in between homes.

Anna with two of her dogs, Tiger and Cookie, in the backyard of their house on Moenart Street in Detroit in a photograph taken in the late 1950's.

Above is a photograph taken inside Bob's house at Moenart Street on November 15, 1961 that gives a glimpse of it inside. Everyone is seated at the dinner table in the large dining room located in the center of the first floor with the living room behind it. Bob and his wife Delphine are on the right. Anna is in the middle. That is the author as a young boy at the table making the face. John's son John Jr. is to the left of me and his mother, Esther, is on the far left facing the table.

I spent a lot of time visiting Bob's house on Moenart when I was young, sleeping over many times. Most of the family holidays were spent there except the summer ones which were spent at the "cottage" the family built in the

1950's about thirty miles northeast of there in New Baltimore on Anchor Bay.

Bob's house was one of the largest houses on the block with a large living room when you entered, a long vestibule with a player piano in it, a dining room in the middle and two bedrooms off the dining room. The huge kitchen was out back as was an enclosed porch behind it. Part of the kitchen was raised a step and Anna had a rocking chair up there that she called her "throne." The bathroom, with the ancient tub sitting on four feet, was off of the kitchen as were the stairs to the large upstairs flat, where the boys slept, and to the full basement. Later after the boys left, Anna would, you guessed it, rent the self-contained upstairs flat to boarders for extra money as she also did with part of the cottage in New Baltimore. Rumor had it that her last husband, Joe Palinski, who I remember as my Grandpa, was one of these boarders who Anna ended up marrying, her fourth time.

Joseph Babiarz's role in this move and reestablishment of the family in Detroit is not clear. What is clear is that John, the oldest child, took on the father's role in the Babaisz family very early, probably when Joseph left Helvetia in 1920, and never lost it. Joseph died on May 15, 1933. Anna married three more times, outliving each of her four husbands, but none of them seemed to play a significant role in Bob's upbringing for some reason. When he was 22 or so, John was hired in the Detroit Fire Department, a plume job that he used to financially support the Babiarz family. It got the Babiarz family through the Great Depression, as John, being a city employee, was never laid off like most workers in private industry were during that time. John retired from the Fire Department in his 60's, having the same job his whole life and rising to Assistant Fire Chief before he retired.

Bob, on the right, with his brother John, sometime in the
1950's. Funny that Bob had a camera as later in life as
when raising his family his wife took all the family photos.

The reason I am telling some of brother John's story
here is that not only did the family survive the Great
Depression because of him but they also had their name
changed to *Babbish* because of him. The story goes that
when it was time for the Fire Department to issue John his

first fireman's paycheck, the paymaster didn't get the spelling of his last name right and on the "Pay to the Order of" line of that first City of Detroit paycheck was the name John *Babbish*.

Anna, the financial officer of the family, upon seeing this mistake when John presented her with the check (all paychecks went to Anna to use to support the family, she kindly giving a dollar or so out of it to the kid who earned it), knew that a bird in the hand was worth two in the bush and had John endorse it exactly as it was made out so as to avoid any controversy at the city and then promptly used part of the paycheck to legally have their named changed to *Babbish*. It was easier to do that than to try to correct it with the City. Any way, that spelling was roughly the way Babiarz was pronounced so who cared? They were also probably mad at Joseph and were glad to be able to disassociate themselves from him at this point, as it seems that he was now out of the picture.

While we are talking about siblings of Bob, we may as well elaborate a bit on them all here as, to know Bob's life story, you need to know the Babbish family.

Frank, the second oldest, who died in 1965 (the first funeral I ever attended), had Anna's knack for entrepreneurship. He at one time worked for the Detroit Street Railway department of the City of Detroit, like his father did, with the job as a motorman running the streetcars. Bob said Frank gave all the ladies a free ride on his streetcar. He also was instrumental in the family owning the gas station on McNichols just up the street from their house on Moenart Street as well as an ice cream shop on McNichols at Davison that was an early seller of soft ice cream, then known as frozen custard. All the kids helped work at these two businesses as they supported the family. This entrepreneurship of Frank lasted his whole life as in a wartime letter Bob wrote to John he inquired as to what new business ventures Frank was up to while Bob was in Europe. Frank also owned a bar later in life (he called it a "beer garden") and his wife Rosie (same name as Bob's sister) ran the beer garden for years after Frank's untimely death. Frank was a very good tennis player and was in the Merchant Marines for a while.

Walter, also known by the nickname "Buck" (he was a big Buck Rogers fan back then), was a gifted accordion player and worked at an auto plant.

Rose, or Rosie as she was called, was younger than Bob and, like Bob, was a gifted athlete, especially playing golf. She worked as a seamstress for Chrysler and was the original "Rosie the Riveter" as she started working in the auto plants during World War II when the men were all off to fight the war. Her husband Joe was, as once described to me by Bob, a "radical" because he was instrumental in organizing and participating in many of the United Auto Workers Union famed sit-down strikes in Detroit and Flint back then.

Chester was the baby of the family and also a gifted athlete, his game being tennis. During World War II Chet was stationed in the South Pacific on a PT boat and later was in navel intelligence after the War. Chet was the second Babbish to attend college, after Bob, and Bob helped him get a sport scholarship to the University of Detroit where he also went to school.

As you can see, in order for the Babbish family to survive, not only in Pennsylvania but also in Detroit, the family had to stick together and work together. Everything done was for Babbish Enterprise, a scheme that no one complained about. Selfishness was not a word that any Babbish understood. This trait lasted Bob's entire life, as he would give anyone the shirt off his back if they asked.

Living on Moenart Street probably turned out to be the major influence on Bob's love of sports, including golf. This was because the house on Moenart Street backed up against not only Lasky Park, a city park a block in size, but also a huge Detroit Department of Recreation playfield known as Jayne Playfield. This huge open area was also part of an elementary school known as White Elementary School and a middle school known as Cleveland Middle School. Between these four occupants this property seemed to stretch for miles and Bob's house was on the northeast corner of it. Bob attended both of these schools.

Behind the alley in back of Bob's house was a long line of tennis courts in Jayne Playfield. This was where Bob as well as brothers Frank and Chester and sister Rose learned to play tennis. I can just see the Babbish kids, after chores or after school, grabbing their tennis rackets (I wonder where they got them from?) and running out the back door of the house and across their small back yard, going across the alley to the gate at the corner of the alley and Luce Street that went into Lasky Park, Jayne Playfield and the tennis courts. Then I can imagine them becoming very serious while they played and learned the game of tennis, playing each other in doubles, fighting who will have Rosie on their team, as she was the girl, or Chester, the best player though the youngest.

Immediately behind the tennis courts was a very large open field. This was where young Bob honed his golf shots, both long and short ones, after he picked up golf in 1926. I am getting a bit ahead of myself here but you get the gist of my story: Bob's family life and the location of his home on Moenart Street were very important to his life as a golfer, husband and father. The move to Detroit changed everything for Bob and his family and gave each of them opportunities that they would have never had in

Pennsylvania, opportunities that they all took advantage of as they were old enough now to realize the break they got.

And this is the sub-theme throughout the life story of Bob Babbish; that the Babbish family made the huge move from countryside to urban life and had the insight to see the opportunities that Detroit opened up for them. Necessity to feed six kids was the overriding concern for Anna but instead of despair it became opportunity for each of her children. A great free education was available that all the kids took advantage of. The resources of a major city like parks and businesses and public golf courses and transportation were tools in their hands to be enjoyed and used because nothing like this existed in Helvetia, Pennsylvania. Nothing about Detroit was taken for granted by the Babbish kids.

And Detroit was just coming into its golden years in the 1920's. The automotive industry was creating a middle class there and the middle class was paying taxes that poured money into an enlightened city that was using this revenue to build the greatest city on earth. Other industries were rapidly forming in Detroit to support the automobile revolution and created more and more jobs. Mass transportation to move all these people around was built, as were roads and expansion of the city limits to accommodate more housing. And Detroit, because of this prosperity, was the city of single-family dwellings. Instead of apartments and housing projects being developed, houses, sturdy and expensive brick houses like the Babbish one on Moenart, were built by the new middle class living and working there, requiring more and more land to accommodate the spread of the population.

The move to Detroit was working out pretty well the first few years. Though the poverty they endured was lessened and there was plenty of food on the table as a result of Babbish Enterprises, this all suddenly came to an end with the advent of the Great Depression in 1929.

Asked once what he remembered most about the Great Depression, Bob replied, "Being hungry." Like all businesses, Babbish Enterprises, the gas station and ice cream stand, were hit hard. Sometimes the Babbish kids would have to walk to the railroad freight yard located about a mile away to try to find and collect sugar beets to eat that had fallen out of hopper cars bringing them down from Michigan's Thumb area where they were grown. One time Bob was doing so and was caught by a railroad cop who threatened to beat him if he didn't drop the beets and leave. Bob looked at the cop in the eye and said that if he doesn't bring the beets home he and the others in his family may starve, so go ahead, beat him over the beets, as he wasn't going to put them down. The cop let him go.

Anna, realizing that her family was in trouble, resorted to a business that had saved them before: she assembled the alcohol still in the basement on Moenart and fired it up! Not having lost her touch, she became the preferred corn whiskey moonshiner in Detroit. Anna's list of customers reportedly included the Mayor of Detroit and the Police Commissioner. Anna again used her innate ingenuity to save the Babbish family in a crisis and the cash they received in whiskey sales got them through the Great Depression. It also helped that in a few years John would be hired by the Detroit Fire Department and have a steady paycheck coming in to give to Anna.

The last story about the moonshining division of Babbish Enterprises was that, at some point, like in Helvetia, it became too well known in Detroit and the Feds were sniffing it out irrespective of the efforts of her customers trying to keep it going and secret. Eventually the Feds showed up at Moenart and busted Anna. Anna put on her immigrant act, only speaking in broken English, crying, begging them not to take her to jail, that she will stop, etc. It worked as they took her word that she would cease and desist making corn whiskey and left.

But, as Anna related the story to me years ago, she had just purchased a 50-pound bag of sugar, which she hadn't even opened, and what could she do with all that sugar? She couldn't let it go to waste, that was not the Babbish way. So she decided to fire up the still one more time only as long as needed to use up this sugar supply.

A week later, with the still snorting away full blast in the basement, there was a pounding on the front door. It was the Feds again. Busted and this time it was serious. The Feds started grabbing Anna to put her in the paddy wagon to take to the federal lockup downtown. Jail! Gathering all her wits about her, she said that they cannot possible take her, the mother of six children, all living at home, to jail. Who would take care of them? When the Feds didn't seem concerned about this she then showed her trump card: "Instead of me, take my son!" Turns out Bob was the only kid home that day. This they did and Bob spent one night in jail for moonshining, a charge that somehow Anna was able to get dropped the next day, probably with a little gift to the Federal Marshall downtown. That was the last of the moonshining, or so Anna said. The Great Depression was just about done by then anyway.

Another story about Bob and Babbish Enterprises and how everyone chipped in to help the family back then relates to one of Bob's first jobs. It was at Dodge Brothers' car manufacturing plant called Dodge Main in Hamtramck, just a few miles west of his house on Moenart. This must have been a high school job for him, probably part time or during the summer. Whatever he did there at that time, when he got his first paycheck it was a big one.

Anna had told him to come straight home with it and be careful, that there were a lot of mean people who might try to rob him of it.

Bob had this in mind and he was so scared on the way home that day that he walked down the middle of the streets so as not to be robbed by someone coming out between the buildings and houses.

Before he got home, though, he came across a bunch of guys he recognized from the plant on the side of the street. They were playing something. Knowing them and feeling safe he came up to see what they were doing. They were playing dice, something Bob knew a little about from his older brothers.

One of the guys, knowing it was payday, asked Bob if he would like to double or triple the amount of money in his paycheck? Thinking that this would really impress Anna, he took the bait. Needless to say, after playing dice with these older sharks Bob went home empty-handed that day. Anna really laid into Bob for this. He had learned his lesson out on the street and, like many things in his life, Bob turned this event into a good thing: he never gambled again. Even when playing golf Bob never wagered more than a couple dollars at a time even though eventually he could afford to wager much more.

# CHAPTER 3
## CADDYING AND HIGH SCHOOL: 1926 TO 1933

Immediately upon moving to Moenart Street in Detroit in 1922, Bob, having just turned seven years old, started first grade at White Elementary School located just at the end of his block. This was the beginning of his formal education that would culminate in Bob becoming the first Babbish/Babiarz/Krupa ever to go to and graduate from college.

A photo of Bob's grade school, White Elementary, in 2015.

Anna knew that the only way her children would break out of the poverty she grew up in and struggled with even then was through education. And now, living in Detroit gave them the opportunity to do so through the great public school system that was being developed at this time.

However, what with the odd-jobs Bob had to do to support his family, studying for school wasn't always at the top of the list of his things to do. Bob was an average student in elementary school at White, graduating from fifth grade there in 1926.

For middle school, Bob went to nearby Cleveland Middle School, located on Conant in the southwest corner of the huge school/recreational rectangle located behind his house on Moenart. He could just cut diagonally across Lasky Park/Jayne Playfield from the alley behind his house to walk the seven blocks to Cleveland. Cleveland was one of those new, huge schools built in Detroit at that time and was very impressive to see. Bob graduated from ninth grade at Cleveland in 1930.

Cleveland Middle School as it appeared in 2015.

In September 1930 Bob went to Northwestern High School on West Grand Boulevard in Detroit as that was the high school in his school zone on Moenart. In 1931 Pershing High School was built on Seven Mile Road and that was the school he transferred to as being the one now in his school zone. He attended Pershing its first year in operation as a junior and graduated a year later in 1933. More on his days at Pershing in a bit as they were very important to Bob and, you guessed it, his golf.

The summer between graduation from elementary school and starting middle school turned out to be the pivotal time in Bob's future. And it was all because of a job he got in 1926.

During this period of time, the sport of golf had reached a crescendo of popularity in the United States. By then it was what could be called golf's "second generation" in America as the players from Scotland and England who introduced it here in the late 1800's and made it famous had been replaced by a new, home-grown generation of American-born golfers to make it America's own. Public and private golf clubs were being built all over the United States to meet the demand of the citizens and Detroit was no exception. At this time Detroit was completing a massive project building public golf courses, or "links," as part of its public recreation department. Everyone was playing and talking about this relatively new game that had gone from being a sport of the privileged to one of the masses, largely because of the public links program in cities like Detroit.

You can see how Bob would have known about golf at such a young age. Though there was no public course real close to them on Moenart, there was Lasky Park and Jayne Playfield out back. But those didn't come into play with Bob right away, as he was too busy with school and working odd jobs for Babbish Enterprises. Not surprisingly, Bob became introduced to golf because of work.

For reasons lost to memory, Bob picked up a job in 1926 as a golf caddy. Maybe it was because he was interested in golf already. Maybe Anna made him. Whatever the reason, this job changed Bob's life forever.

Back in 1926 there were plenty of private golf courses in and all around Detroit, some not too far away from Bob's home on Moenart, that hired caddies to carry the members' clubs. Again, for reasons lost to memory, or maybe for reasons related to a young man's wish for adventure, Bob started caddying at Orchard Lake Country Club in Orchard Lake, Michigan.

Located about 25 miles northwest of his house on Moenart, Orchard Lake Country Club was really out in the country back in 1926. Public transportation only went so far back then and the way Bob got to his new job as a caddy out there is a great story and indicative of how creative and adventurous he was.

As Bob tells the story, he and a friend caddied there on weekends after they started the school term that fall. They left on a Friday afternoon, skipping the afternoon classes to get to the Club by mid-afternoon. They borrowed some pocket change from Anna to pay the bus and interurban fares to get there, using some of the money they earned caddying to pay their way back.

In order to get to Orchard Lake Country Club, Bob and his friend had to take a city bus down McNichols Road for four miles to Woodward Avenue. Once on Woodward they caught an interurban train car operated by Detroit United Rail that went north to Pontiac. Getting off the DUR interurban at 18 Mile Road in Bloomfield Hills, they stuck out their thumbs and hitchhiked the seven or so miles along Long Lake Road, as 18 Mile Road was called, to Orchard Lake Road on the east banks of Orchard Lake. Then they had to go an additional couple of miles on Pontiac Trail and Orchard Trail (one-time Indian trails) to Orchard Lake Country Club, usually having to walk those last couple of miles.

Bob was quoted in one of the newspaper articles about him that reminisced about his caddying days at Orchard Lake Country Club as saying that, "Hitchhiking out there from the east side of Detroit in those days was tough – no traffic. But we used to do it even if it took all day."

I once pointed out to Bob that on the way to Orchard Lake he passed at least five other golf courses he could have caddied at that were much closer to his home: Detroit Golf Club on McNichols, Red Run Golf Club in Royal Oak, Birmingham Golf Club in Birmingham, Bloomfield Hills Golf Club (he saw its fairways from Long Lake Road on the way) and Pine Lake Country Club in West Bloomfield Township. Bob said that he didn't recall why they picked Orchard Lake. Maybe they heard that it was looking for caddies and the others were not at the time. Anyway, caddying at Orchard Lake made for an adventure, which is the real reason I believe he went there.

The goal was always to try to get to the golf club as early as possible on Friday afternoon in order to try to get a late caddying job carrying the clubs of a member sneaking out after work.

Bob said that Friday night they slept in a barn somewhere around the golf course (it was still all agricultural around it back then) and woke up early Saturday morning hoping for two loops, one in the morning and one in the afternoon.

After sleeping a second night in a barn on Saturday, the boys would catch a Sunday morning loop and then have to start heading back home in the afternoon, as Anna wanted Bob home for dinner. The boys would splurge and spend some of their hard-earned caddy earnings on a hamburger at the famous Wilkins Inn, located at the corner of Orchard Lake Road and Pontiac Trail, then retrace their journey back to Detroit as they had come two days earlier.

Bob said that the first time he ever picked up or even saw a golf club was that first day caddying at Orchard Lake Country Club in 1926. The thrill of the adventure getting there to caddy, the beauty of the country club setting, the class and social standing of the golfers, the intricacies of the game, these were the things that impressed this eleven-year-old boy about the sport of golf. That first day caddying set the stage for a life long love of golf for Bob. And the rest is history.

Bob caddied at Orchard Lake for a number of years, sometimes also caddying at closer (by seven hitchhiking miles) Bloomfield Hills Country Club. During this time he also taught himself how to golf. The entire winter of 1926/27 he practiced swinging a club and putting the ball in his basement on Moenart, using some used clubs and balls that generous Orchard Lake members gave him. Remember Lasky Park and Jayne Playfield in his backyard? Those were his driving ranges in the warmer weather where he practiced hitting golf balls whenever he could. Good-bye tennis, hello golf. And this was still all in middle school where they did not have golf as a sport.

Caddying was Bob's entry into the world of golf. By being a worker carrying bags for the golfers, Bob learned the game of golf and could compare the differences in the swings of many different golfers day after day, memorizing the swings of the good golfers and learning from the mistakes of the bad ones. It also allowed him to contribute to Babbish Enterprises with his caddy earnings so he was killing two birds with one ball.

Bob caddied at Orchard Lake four years, until 1930. Like all golf clubs in the area, Orchard Lake participated in the Detroit District Golf Association Caddy Championship held every year and sent its best golfing caddies to compete in it. In just these four years Bob had become a very good golfer by 1930 and Orchard Lake sent him to that year's caddy tournament for the first time. The Orchard Lake team, which he captained, won the caddie team championship that year, the first of many tournament wins for Bob on the golf course. He was 15 years old at the time. Can you imagine the thrill of winning your first golf tournament at that age and after playing only four years?

In 1931 in his first year Pershing High School and 16-years-old Bob got smart (or maybe he was recruited) and started caddying at the Detroit Golf Club which was only about five miles from his house. The caddy superintendent at DGC, Hugh T. Syron, Jr., just happened to be the one who conducted the caddy tournaments so maybe the recruiting theory is the correct one.

In an article published in The Detroit News dated August 23, 1932 written by John Walter (the writer who sent Bob photocopies of many old Detroit News articles on him in 1972 before he retired from the newspaper), the 1932 Detroit District Golf Association Caddie Championship was described. Bob was still playing for DCG and this was his last caddie tournament because of his age. Teams from 15 golf clubs competed that year and it was held at Meadowbrook Country Club in Northville. Two separate championships were played then: The team championship and the individual championship.

That year DGC won the team championship with an aggregate score of 497 for the six players for 18 holes. Bob was on this team for the first time.

For the third consecutive year a youth from another club had won the individual championship by having the low score that day. It was Harry Albrecht of Gowanie Golf Club who shot a 77, one stroke lower than Bob's 78.

However, Bob's caddy superintendent at DGC, Hugh

Syron, Jr., who was again running the tournament, got word from someone that Harry was too old to compete that year as he was now 18 years old and the cut-off was 17. Looking at Harry's application it said he was 17. By chance, Hugh had Harry's application from the year before and it too said he was 17 years old last year. The new application also required a birthdate and on it was January 15, 1915. According to that he was 17 years old again! Something was amiss and old Hugh was going to smoke it out. I am sure it had nothing to do with Bob coming in second place in the individual championship that tournament.

The article continued that to settle the matter Hugh made a "flying trip" to Mount Clemens that afternoon, the county seat where Harry Albrecht was born, and consulted the birth records on file there. His birth certificate showed that he was born in 1914 and so was really 18 years old and thus ineligible to play in the caddie championship that year. This gave Bob the individual title and DGC its first individual champion in three years.

In later years, caddy master Hugh Syron rated Bob as one of the best boys who ever worked for him and certainly the best golfer of the batch.

Bob used to tell the story of how he once caddied for the famous woman athlete Babe Didrikson at Orchard Lake Country Club. As he was the best caddy there at the time the caddie superintendent assigned him to carry Babe's bags that day of her visit. At that point Babe was a great track and field athlete, winning gold medals in the upcoming 1932 Olympics in Los Angeles, but had not made her name as a golfer yet.

Back when Bob started playing golf in his middle school days in the late 1920's they were still playing with wooden-shafted clubs. Many of the irons, instead of having a number, had a name. There was the "mashie niblick" which was a seven iron, the "niblick" which was a nine iron, the "jigger," which was a short-shafted iron used for long low chips to the hole from just off the green, among others. Even the woods had names back then like the "brassie," which was a two-wood, one of Bob's favorites, and a "spoon," which was a four wood, another club Bob excelled at using. Many of the newspaper articles back then used these names when describing what club he used on a certain shot. I often remember Bob calling clubs by these names when I played with him in the 1970's as a young man and I even sometimes used a jigger Bob still owned. I recall in his bag of extra clubs he still had a wooden-shafted putter that was one of his favorites though I rarely recall him ever use it, preferring his slender, brass Titleist putter or funny hollow Ping putter in later years.

When Bob started Pershing High School in the fall of 1931, his second of three years of high school, the first year being at Northwestern High School as Pershing was not open yet, he was immediately attracted to all the sports there, not just golf. He weighed only 130 pound back then, a bit on the light side for his height of 5' 10" that he had achieved by that time. Bob concentrated on three sports while at Pershing. In the fall he played on the golf team and more on that later. In the winter he played hockey and in the spring baseball.

Bob really liked hockey. He was a defenseman for Pershing in the City Hockey League. They played at the old Olympia Stadium on the City's west side, then home of the Detroit Red Wings professional hockey club. Asked why he played defense, Bob replied that he never could learn to lift the puck and so he couldn't be a forward as he was never able to score goals. Remember, the curved hockey stick was still thirty years in the future. In 1932, the

City dropped the Hockey League, probably because of the Great Depression, and Bob decided to forget hockey and concentrate instead on…. baseball??

Yes, baseball. Bob was the star pitcher and hitter on the Pershing High School baseball team for two years. Naturally ambidextrous, Bob was a switch-hitter at the plate and powerful on both sides. Not to hide his ambidextrous skills on the mound, Bob would pitch right-handed to left-handed batters to get that advantage, wearing a right-handed mitt on his appropriate left hand. But when a right-handed batter came to the plate, Bob would put the mitt on his right hand backwards or just throw it on the dirt on the mound and pitch left-handed!

Bob taught me how to ice skate. When I was seven years old we went to a small lake close to our house in the suburbs. Bob put on an ancient pair of ice skates, helped me strap on mine, and off we went skating on Gilbert Lake with me between his legs trying to stand straight on my skates. I was amazed at how well Bob skated that day and he taught me how to skate before we were done.

Bob also taught me how to play baseball. At around the same age he took me out back and we started throwing a baseball. He told me how to catch it properly in the mitt and how to pitch it so that the batter didn't see the ball coming until it left my hand. He would only throw me the ball underhanded, saying he didn't want to pull a muscle throwing it overhand and affect his golf game. But as I write this I wonder if his baseball days in high school were really playing what we now call "softball" and that he pitched underhand instead of overhand? There is a newspaper article touching upon his baseball days at Pershing and it did say "baseball" instead of "softball" but maybe they didn't make a written distinction between the two back then.

If caddying was the first step in Bob's life of golf, Pershing High School was the second step. Immediately named the captain of the school's first golf team, Bob's reputation preceding him and he didn't disappoint his coach, Ray Huffman.

Above is a picture of Bob on the right in his letter sweater at Pershing High School with his coach Ray Huffman in the center and fellow golfer Harry Stimson on the left. This photograph was published in 1932 in a local Detroit newspaper with the following caption: "Virtually every chronic golfer in Detroit would like to shoot the kind of golf these two youngsters turn in every day as star members of the Pershing High School golf team. Robert Babbish occasionally equals par. He is always within a few strokes of it. Harry Stimson is a couple of strokes behind him. Their coach, Ray Huffman, is proud of them. That's why they are smiling."

Below is another Pershing photograph of Bob, again with Harry Stimson who was the only other player on the team those first two years of golf at the new high school.

The preceding two photos were the first photographs taken
of Bob. Being from a poor family in the early part of the
20<sup>th</sup> Century, you couldn't afford to hire a professional
photographer to photograph your family. High school
usually brought the first photo; the graduation photo.
Above is Bob's Pershing Class of 1933 graduation photo.

HIGH SCHOOL GOLFERS SWING INTO TITLE PLAY

BIAGIO DI BLASI                    ROBERT BABBISH

HARRY STIMSON

Di Blasi, captain of Redford's team, will defend the individual title Saturday in the twelfth annual City High School Golf Championship Tournament at Washtenaw Country Club. Babbish and Stimson, of Pershing, and Thack, of Mackenzie, are expected to be his chief rivals. More than 133 golfers representing 16 high schools will participate in 18-hole competition for the team title now held by Redford.

To finish off the caddying and high school years of Bob we have, as seen above, another newspaper article about the 1932 twelfth annual City High School Golf Championship Tournament at Washtenaw Country Cub near Ann Arbor. Biagio Di Blasi of Redford High, seen in the upper left, was the defending champ. Pershing High, with Bob (upper right) and teammate Stimson (lower), hoped to dethrone him. Bob did that year. Golf at all levels caught the public's attention and the local newspapers in Detroit covered it all very well back then.

# CHAPTER 4
## THE GREAT BABBISH: 1933 TO 1938

I borrowed the title of this chapter from a 1972 letter to Bob from The Detroit News writer John Walter. The first sentence in the letter said, "Here are a few more copies of clippings of The Great Babbish." John should know as he covered Bob's golf career from its beginnings in 1932. And certainly Bob was at his greatest between the years 1933 to 1938, culminating in winning his first and only national championship.

When Bob graduated from Pershing High School in 1933 he had led his high school golf team to the Detroit City League tournament victory that prior autumn in 1932. His caddying and high school golf successes were the warm-up to what would be his greatest two periods of golf, those years covered in this chapter and the years while he was in college that will be covered in the next chapter.

Like most poor boys during the Great Depression, and we are still in it during this chapter of Bob's life, their families were struggling to stay alive. The Babbish family was hungry during this time and enough money had to be scrapped together to keep food on the table and bills paid. Older son John had yet to land his Detroit Fire Department job and all the kids were chipping in to do odd jobs to keep the family going. Bob, even with his golf talents, had to do his part.

What this meant was that going to college was out of the question even though it would have been the next logical step for Bob. There was no money to pay for college and probably no one in the Babbish family even thought of going to college because poor families didn't back then.

Even when golf was one's profession it usually didn't pay enough money to support most golfers back then. Many people asked Bob why he didn't become a professional golfer, especially during this period of time when he was at his peak. Bob always answered, "Because there was no money in it." He used to tell me that the pros made more money on their side bets during a tournament than they did winning the tournament. And, as we know, Bob did not gamble.

Being a professional golfer back in the 1930's did not mean being able to make a living at it. The tournament prize money was meager if you won and usually not enough to even pay your entrance fee and travel expenses in playing if you came in second or third place, often the only other positions to receive any prize money. To win $500 for first place would have been a big prize back then. If you were a pro lucky enough to work at a golf club you would be making some money at that and some for giving golfing lessons but still often not enough to make a living. It was usually a part-time job for them.

Plus there was still a class distinction between being a professional golfer and an amateur. Many looked down on the poor souls that had to golf for a living as opposed to those who golfed because they loved the game. Now, you would think that this wouldn't make much difference to the gifted golfer like Bob who was dirt poor anyway. Why not make a living out of a sport you love when there was no apparent downside to doing so? Bob saw it differently, though, and he had the insight to see that he could make a living as an amateur golfer by using golf as a springboard for being a businessman. More on that later.

Above is a photograph of Bob (left) with his lifelong golf friend Chick Harbert (right) playing golf sometime in the mid-1930's, probably at a tournament. Chick went on to become a very accomplished professional golfer, winning the PGA Tournament in 1954 and a club pro for years.

As an aside, on May 15, 1933, Bob's father Joseph Babiarz passed away. This would have been around the date of Bob's graduation from Pershing High School. Bob never spoke about his father other than to say he was a coal miner and left alone for Detroit in 1920 to find a better life for his family. This leads one to think that Joseph must have left Anna (or Anna kicked him out - I wouldn't put it past her) and abandoned the family sometime between 1920 and his death and became a non-entity to them. Being Catholic, divorce was out of the question. It is interesting, though, that Bob remembered the date of his death. Another mystery that is buried with the Babbish family.

I once asked Bob what he did in these years between high school and college. He said that he was a "golf bum." When asked to clarify, Bob said that whenever he could he would play in some golf tournament somewhere in the United States. When asked how he could afford to, it being in the middle of the Great Depression, Bob replied that he and his golf friends would "beg, borrow and steal" to get the money for the entrance fees, the gas to drive there, to pay for a place to stay, etc. Where he found the time to do so and also provide for the Babbish family is a mystery but he must have had his mother Anna's blessing as well as the support of his family. They probably all recognized that they had a great one in the family, someone that may reach the American dream of using his talent to bring themselves out of poverty and to a better life.

If Bob was playing in a big tournament the newspapers back then covered it. But many of the tournaments were smaller ones, local in nature and not making the sports pages of the newspapers. This is why we do not know much about this period of time in Bob's life. Sure there were probably newspaper articles in the local towns where the tournaments were played but no one from the family got those newspapers to clip the articles out and save them. I got the impression that Bob played in a golf tournament somewhere in the United States every weekend for most of these years. He told me that first and foremost he would try to find someone to sponsor him for a tournament. This meant paying the entrance fee, travel money and a place to stay. These sponsors were sometimes individuals trying to encourage a young gifted golfer to pursue his sport or other times a golf club or business. Hard to say where the line was drawn to slip into becoming a professional golfer but Bob never crossed that line. (He once told me that his fellow amateur, Chick Harbert, once received some money for winning a tournament as an amateur and, like a police officer seeing a crime in progress, the professional golf association contacted him the next day and said to give the money back or he would be considered a professional. Chick's reply to them was, "Well, I guess I am a professional now." Chick had a very successful career.)

During his golf bum days, Bob often was able to stay at the house of some member of the sponsoring golf club, often from contacts back in Detroit. He would travel with many of his fellow golf buddies to these events so they could share a car and expenses getting there. They often went from one tournament to another without a trip home to save on money. All to satisfy their love of playing golf in the most competitive situations possible. Bob kept in touch with most of his fellow golf bums from then his entire life, some of which turned pro, like Chick Harbert and Bob Gajda, and others who remained amateurs. It seems like all of them continued to play golf their entire lives as Bob did (he played regularly until he was 94).

But back to The Great Babbish. What we do know about this period of time was that in 1933 Bob won his first non-caddying or school golf tournament: the Public Links Tournament held at Bob 'O Links Golf Club in Detroit. It was appropriate that this was his first win as he was a product of the Detroit public golf courses. Many great golfers were poor boys and girls with talent who were provided a place to learn and perfect their skills on the public golf courses in Detroit. This was another great resource to the Babbish family in moving to Detroit that Bob and others in his family were able to take advantage of.

In 1934 Bob became a member of the Beverly Hills Country Club. How he could afford this is a mystery. It had to have been paid by a sponsor or been offered a free membership because of his golfing skills and the fame Bob would bring to the club. Back then in order to play in the U.S. Amateur tournament you had to be a member of a club that was affiliated with one of the national governing golf bodies and so we have to presume this was why Bob felt compelled to join one. It is a story in itself of the American Dream that Bob, until recently a caddy and right out of high school, was now a member of a golf club.

What Bob always considered to be his first "major" golf tournament win was the 1934 Detroit District Golf Association's Open-Amateur championship held at Bonnie Brook Golf club on July 13, 1934. Bonnie Brook was located on the city's far northwest corner at Telegraph and Eight Mile Roads. When I was young we used to drive by it fairly often and Bob would always say, "That's where I won my first golf tournament." I just drove by Bonnie Brook the other day (it is no longer a golf course and is vacant and overgrown now) and told my wife, Elaine, "That's where Dad won…"

John Walter of The Detroit News, who coined the phrase "The Great Babbish," wrote this tournament up in the July 13, 1934 edition of the paper. The article notes that the first 36 holes of the tournament was also the qualifying round for playing in that year's National Public Links championship from July 30 to August 4 in Pittsburgh and, "No sooner than Bob had been selected a member of the Detroit team for that event, he further proved that he was entitled to that position by winning the 72-hole Michigan Open-Amateur the next 36 holes. In the first round of the finals Bob shot a 72, two over par, and then finished with a 70 to withstand the challenge of many sharp-shooters on the final round, giving him a total of 287 strokes, three strokes ahead of Larry O'Palka, two-time Open-Amateur champion.

"Bob had a one-stroke lead at the start of the final two rounds. Then Bill Fenwick of Western Golf Club came through with a 68, two under par, to share the lead with him at 54 holes. It was then that Bob came through with some of his most sensational golf of the day to end the challengers' threats on the first three holes of the final round."

John Walter described it: "Bob's drive went into the creek on the first hole but he laid his approach 12 feet from the pin and holed the putt to get his par. He then holed a 20-foot putt on the second hole for a birdie three. On the 330-yard third hole Bob hit his best drive of the tournament, the ball stopping on the edge of the green and he chipped up for one putt to put him two under par for the first three holes, giving him a lead that he never relinquished."

As to Bob playing in the National Public Links championship that year in Pittsburgh, he went to the third round before being eliminated. As mentioned, it was his first start in a national competition. He held the Number 1 position of Detroit's team of players competing in it that year. David A. Mitchell was the winner. The point here being that The Great Babbish was on the national golf scene at the age of 19 years old in 1934.

Also in 1934 Bob played in the Michigan Amateur Golf Tournament for the first time. It was held at the Country Club of Lansing and Bob was runner-up to his friend Chuck Kocsis.

The year 1934 was Bob's breaking out year in golf. He had proved himself in high school and made the step to adult amateur golf, both at the state and national level, without any problem and to no one's surprise. And he did this while still helping to support the family in the middle of the Great Depression with odd jobs and working at the family gas station and ice cream shop.

Bob's golfing successes continued with the start of the 1935 season. That year he joined Brooklands Golf and Country Club in Rochester, Michigan (now known as the Rochester Hills Golf and Country Club) and played out of there for the next eleven years.

The Detroit District Golf Association, predecessor to the Michigan Golf Association, was formed in 1919 by 14 golf clubs in Detroit and Windsor, Ontario. Its premier golfing event for years was its annual Detroit District Championship held at a different District course each year.

Bob first played in the Detroit District Championship in 1935 and he reached the semifinals that year. That was his warm-up for the next tournament, the Michigan Amateur.

The 1935 Michigan Amateur Golf Tournament was held at Belvedere Golf Club in the northern Michigan town of Charlevoix. In an article written by Lloyd Northard for one of the three Detroit newspapers dated July 22, 1935, it said that, "Bob had to rally late on the final nine holes of the tournament after blowing a safe lead that had been wiped out by Edward J. Novak, a collegian from Traverse City. With the match square and with only three holes to play, Bob sank putts of 14 and 10 feet to win two holes and the match 2 to 1 over Novak" to win the Michigan Amateur Championship Tournament.

The article went on to say that no new state champion ever was more pleased than Bob. "I thought I had tossed my chance away when I began stabbing my putts," Bob was quoted as saying afterwards. "I don't know why I did it but it was leaving me impossible second putts. When I came to the seventeenth I was almost in a daze. At first I wanted to play an easy spoon shot. Then I figured the breeze wasn't as strong as in the morning so I took a mid-iron. I knew I was going to hook the shot but instead of playing for the banks at the right of the green, I hit straight at the pin and the hook carried the ball down the hill.

"I thought I had lost my lead right there but Novak, evidently trying to hold back on his iron, hit the ball too softly and was far short of the green. Right then I took hold of myself, knowing I had a chance that might never come again. I was sure of that last putt all the way." Bob continued, "I think I should send telegrams to Chuck [Kocsis] and Chris [Brinke] thanking them for not coming [out to play in it] this year."

The article said that Bob set a new record by playing every long tee shot with his "spoon," or four-wood, instead of his driver. He had been hooking too much with his driver and decided he must make a change if he was to make it past the first round. Supposedly he also played the last three rounds with the same ball instead of switching to a new one for each round. [Editor's Note: he probably couldn't afford another ball.] The article also said that Bob upset the contention that the qualifying medalist [lowest score in the qualifying rounds] never wins the Michigan Amateur, something that had been the case up to this point. He had led the qualifiers with a one under par 71.

The newspaper article went into a hole-by-hole description of Bob's final two rounds of the tournament. "The first hole was his favorite as he scored birdie three's there in both the morning and afternoon rounds after being outdriven many yards by Novak and those two birdies provided Bob's winning margin. In the morning he rolled in a seven-foot putt and in the afternoon a 25-footer.

"But Bob couldn't hold the lead and at the third hole drove his drive into a bank along a trout stream that crossed the fairway and put his third shot over the green, getting a double bogey to Novak's par. Novak dropped a 12-foot putt for a birdie on the fifth and was one up.

"Novak missed the sixth green and lost the hole to Bob's par four and Bob again took the lead when Novak buried his drive in the creek bank on the seventh hole. Then Bob's putter saved him for the scored pars and gained halves through single puts on the eighth and ninth to turn one up.

"Bob missed his drive on the eleventh and put his third over the green to lose the hole after they had halved the tenth with birdies. A second shot that stopped four feet from the pin gave Novak a birdie three and the lead again at the twelfth. A stymie [Bob's ball blocking Novak's line to the hole] forced Novak to take three putts at the fourteenth and Bob came back even. Then Bob tried to drive across the corner of the dogleg fifteenth and it dropped among the trees. Although he made a sensational shot from there [Editor's Note: Bob was always best when in trouble] across the fairway he didn't have a chance as Novak had an easy birdie to go one up.

"Then Bob rallied and with two birdies and a par ended the morning round by winning the last three holes to lead 2 up. He ran down an eight-foot putt at the sixteenth for a three and followed with a five-footer for a two at the seventeenth. Bob drove to the rough on the eighteenth but Novak didn't get his second out and sliced his third almost across a road, the ball stopping in a dry ditch. Bob's third shot was four feet from the cup and Novak conceded the putt. Bob finished with a 38 for the front nine and a 35 for the back for a 73."

The newspaper article then continued with a blow-by-blow account of the afternoon's final round in the 1935 Michigan Amateur tournament. "Bob started his afternoon running his lead to 4 up with his birdie on the first hole and par on the second after Novak topped his second shot. Novak reclaimed a hole at the third by sinking a 12-foot putt. Bob missed by a half an inch of getting his birdie three and a half when his ball held up on the lip of the cup. Novak made Bob a gift of the fifth hole because his first two drives hooked out of bounds. Bob also played it badly, getting a double bogey six, one less than Novak's triple bogey. They halved the next two holes, leaving Bob with a 4 up lead with eleven holes to play.

"Then came Novak's rally and the surprising collapse of Bob's short game, which he always excelled in. Bob put his tee shot over the eighth green and his chip was short. Novak rolled in a 10-foot birdie to win the ninth hole and was only two down. Bob then hooked his drive and pushed his second shot while Novak's second successive birdie four left him only one down at the tenth.

"Novak's rally was halted temporarily at the eleventh where Bob made a sensational second shot from the rough to within eight feet of the cup and holed the putt for a birdie three. Bob's second shot on the twelfth was on the green while Novak's was off to the left. But instead of winning the hole Bob tossed it away with three putts to

# New Golfing Threat

Photo of Bob after winning the 1935 Michigan Amateur

Novak's one putt. On the next hole Bob hooked his drive into the rough and put the second shot over the thirteenth green and Novak again won the hole with a one putt and the match was now square with five holes to go.

"They halved the par three fourteenth hole even though they both had a bogey, Bob three-putting after hitting the green and Novak missing the green and still having to two-putt. They also halved the fifteenth hole, both missing the green with their second shots and remaining even.

"Then Bob came back on the sixteenth and seventeenth holes as he had done in the morning round to win. Bob's second shot on sixteen hit the green but bounced over it. He pitched back 14 feet past the pin. Novak was short of the green with his second shot and his chip just reached the edge of the carpet. Novak's approach was six inches short of the hole but he didn't get a chance to make it as Bob dropped his long putt to win the hole.

"Bob missed the seventeenth green to the left and Novak was short. Bob chipped to within 10 feet of the cup while his opponent's chip was short. Novak's approach putt rolled three feet past the cup and Bob, finally regaining his putting, rapped his 10-footer solidly against the back of the cup to clinch the championship 2 to 1."

We are lucky to have Lloyd Northland's article about the 1935 Michigan Amateur as not too many articles were saved from these early years of Bob's golfing career. As you can see, golf was a big deal in Detroit and elsewhere and the newspapers covered these events, even amateur ones, extensively.

ob Babbish (center), n e w Michigan Open Amateur golf brou
hampion, was only one over par in winning the title Thursday (left
y the aid of some great playing, but he patted his caddy on the at t
ack when he finished and gave him most of the credit. "He at P

Above is another photograph we have of Bob playing in
the 1935 Michigan Amateur Tournament that he won at
the age of 20. The interesting thing about this photo is that
on the left is Bob's baby brother, Chester, who caddied for
him in that tournament.

The year 1936 continued Bob's great golf playing though he did not win any major tournaments. As defending champion of the Michigan Amateur that year he lost to David Ward at the Saginaw Country Club. And again he reached the semifinals at the DDGA District Golf Championship. The Great Depression was starting to wind down by now, taking some pressure off of Bob to come up with money for the family. Plus older brother John was now working for the Detroit Fire Department and bringing home a weekly paycheck to Anna. Brother Frank's gas station that he owned with Bob and brother Walter was doing well and Walter was now a professional accordion player bringing home some money from that.

In 1937 Bob was still hitting his stride as a golfer. He again reached the DDGA District Golf Championship semifinals and again he was runner up in the Michigan Amateur, this time to Chuck Kocsis at Gull Lake Country Club in Kalamazoo. He was also the runner up in the Michigan Open.

Bob's major win in 1937 was the Michigan Open-Amateur, which was the first big tournament he won back in 1934 at Bonnie Brook Golf Club. John Walter wrote an article about this win dated July 9, 1937 for The Detroit News. In it he said that Bob had a 73, one over par, and beat Drew Egleston in a playoff hole. It was held at Rammler Golf Club in Sterling Heights. This duplicated his 1934 victory and he joined only two other players at the time to repeat in the Open-Amateur, a 72-hole medal play tournament.

The same article also had a side story about Bob's 20-year-old sister Rose as well as a picture of her. It said that Bob was going to give her his first prize award, a set of matched golf clubs. It went on to quote the youthful Brooklands golfer as saying, " 'I'd like to see Rose play more golf" and that he had hoped that Rose, an all-around star athlete when she attended Pershing High School, will add further laurels to the Babbish family's golfing prestige. Rose did so over the years. She represented Pershing in interscholastic golf just as Bob did and won many Detroit and Michigan women golf tournaments."

Bob also competed in his first National Amateur Tournament held at the Alderwood Country Club in Portland, Oregon in 1937. For his first round he drew the defending champion, Johnny Fisher, and lost 4-3.

Above and on the next page are two rare photographs of Bob traveling to an out-of-state golf tournament, the 1937 National Amateur Tournament in Portland, Oregon. The photograph above shows Bob and his friends stopping at a scenic mountainous location on the way there from Detroit. It looks like Bob's friend Chick Harbert is the one waving and Bob is on the far right leaning on the car.

Above is a shot of Bob and two of his travel companions at the Alderwood Country Club in Portland, OR in 1937.

The golfing crescendo that was The Great Babbish reached its peak in 1938. By then the Great Depression was pretty much over and the additional financial worries that the Babbish family endured for the last nine years (not that they weren't used to financial worries their entire lives) were almost gone. The gas station up the street from Moenart that Bob was part owner of didn't require his labor as much, giving him more time for golf. Same with the family ice cream store a few blocks away. Bob was now playing 27 to 36 holes of golf a day either in practice rounds or in the many tournaments he played in. His golf bumming days were over as he was a college boy now, the first Babbish to ever be such, entering the University of Detroit in 1936. More on his college days in Chapter 5.

What we were seeing in 1938 was the Great American Dream playing out for Bob. He was on the back nine of it and would soon win the dream that year. Where else could a poor boy, son of a coal miner, have been able to under such horrible economic and to some extent personal circumstances transcend what seemed to have been destined to be a life of poverty to one of fame and even fortune (though not yet) based on his talents alone? Only in America and, maybe at this time in history, only in Detroit.

This does not just happen, though. The person has to take advantage of the possibilities presented to him and use the talents that he may just be discovering to do so. For Bob those possibilities and advantages offered by the City of Detroit at its peak of production and culture, the availability of mass transportation, public parks, golf courses and recreation departments, great public schools, wealth from the new automotive industry that resulted in jobs like caddying for those youngsters that wanted to work, were taken. And they propelled him into a better life that he was able to live the rest of his life and pass onto his children and them to their children.

Of course, this could not have been done without talent. And I am willing to bet that Bob's golf talent would not have been discovered in Helvetia, Pennsylvania. It was discovered, of all places, working as a caddy at a private golf club on a job to help support the family. And, as everyone who knew Bob would tell you, in addition to his golf talent he also had a great, outgoing personality. You couldn't help but like Bob. Everyone was his friend and that went both ways with Bob. Plus he never forgot your name or your story. Bob was truly a remarkable people person. Combine personality with talent and you could go far in the second quarter of the 20th Century.

And don't forget Bob's family in all of this. It would have been very easy for Anna to just say no, forget this golf stuff. That is for rich people, which you aren't and will never be. Go to work in the factory, bring home the bacon so we can survive.

But Anna knew that when a child had talent, no matter in what, it was a gift from God that had to be nurtured and encouraged, no matter how it affected the current state of affairs. They would get by somehow. And the Babbish family did.

And what about the siblings? Were they, when working for Babbish Enterprise to keep the family ship afloat, jealous of Bob and his golf hobby? Sibling pressure is a strong thing and if this were the case Bob would not have been traveling all over the country in the Great Depression playing golf and for free as an amateur. Each Babbish kid had a talent and they were all able to use it to the extent they wanted, whether it was running a business or playing golf, tennis or accordion.

And they all supported each other in their talents. It not

only helped them collectively get through the hard times they were brought up in but made them loving, unselfish people. The phrase "work hard, play hard" could have been coined by the Babbish family. The hard times made them appreciate hard work but you worked hard so you could enjoy life and you made time to enjoy life. Using their talents was the way to enjoy life for the Babbish kids. Bob's biggest cheerleader during this time was his family.

The 1938 golf schedule was a full one for Bob, representing the fact that he was in his prime and the man to beat. His greatest golfing win would occur that August.

Bob qualified for and competed in his first U.S. Open tournament in 1938. This was an accomplishment that all golfers throughout the years dream of doing someday and Bob first accomplished this when he was only 23 years old. That year it was held at Cherry Hill Golf Club in Denver, Colorado. He finished as the fifth low amateur in his first test against the country's greatest golfers, shooting a 322 overall and tied for 55th place, an Open accomplishment that Bob was very proud of, as were his Detroit fans. This was the first of eight U.S. Opens Bob qualified for.

Bob also played for the first time in the National Intercollegiate tournament at the Louisville Country Club in Louisville, Kentucky, where all the best college golfers competed. He was able to play in this tournament as he was in college in 1936.

At this tournament Bob won the quarterfinals 3 to 2 over Willie Turnesa from Holy Cross College. An article in an unknown newspaper said that Bob "thundered" over the Louisville Country Club course with a "spectacular" comeback for the second time in two days there to lead the "high-class" parade into the semifinals and that Turnesa was a favorite to win the tournament. "Babbish, the smooth-stroking Polish boy from Detroit, fired three-under par golf in the afternoon after the Holy Cross star had finished the morning round two-up. Babbish came back in the afternoon to snuff out Turnesa's hopes as the Detroiter carded five threes and a deuce on the 16 holes needed to settle the verdict and finished with a 68 for the day."

Another article in an unknown newspaper said that Bob "squeezed into" the semifinals of this tournament and quickly established himself as the man to beat for the title with Bob being ruled a slight favorite on the basis of his "spectacular" quarterfinal victory even though he was the lowest qualifier for the tournament.

The same article gave another account of Bob's quarterfinal victory over Turnesa. "Turnesa had built up a two-hole lead on the morning round with a one under par 70 against Bob's 71. But Bob fired birdies on the nineteenth and twentieth to pull even and they rounded the turn for the last nine holes even. Pars on the twenty-eighth and thirtieth and a birdie on thirty-three put Bob 3-up and he closed out the match by halving the thirty-fourth hole."

However, in the semifinal round, as writer John Walter stated in an article dated July 3, 1938, "Bob ran into a tartar in John P. Burke, a Georgetown sophomore. Detroiters were visioning their second collegiate titleholder in three years, Babbish's duplication of Chuck Kocsis's 1936 victory, when Burke's birdie (halving the hole) halted the Titan's recovery at the 36th hole and gave Burke the match one up." Titan was the mascot for Bob's college that he was representing, University of Detroit. Not bad a finish for his first time at this event.

I found the following information on that National Intercollegiate Tournament semifinal match in an Associated Press article. "Burke had an early six-up margin and just outlasted Bob for the one-up decision on the thirty-sixth green where Burke matched Bob's birdie for halve to clinch the victory. They played in a steady rain that day and Bob had a 79, eight over par on the morning round while Burke had a 71 to build up that six-hole margin. Bob had cut into this lead by winning the first two holes in the afternoon, sinking a 20-foot putt to take the twentieth. Burke went back five-up at the twenty-fourth hole when Bob missed the green then failed on a 10-foot putt. Bob started the last nine holes four strokes down after winning the twenty-seventh with a par as Burke sent his tee shot into a trap, exploded out of it over the green, then picked up his ball conceding the hole. Bob had Burke on the run when he won thirty, thirty-one and thirty-two as Burke went four-over par on the three holes but recovered to take the thirty-third hole with a par three. Bob took the next hole with a par, they halved thirty-five and, Burke going one-up staring the last hole, pulled out the victory by halving it with Bob."

John Walter went on to say some nice things about Bob in his article. "Always smiling and courteous, Babbish is such a likeable fellow he generally has the galleries pulling for him. That was the case when Kocsis beat him in the 1934 state amateur final. Babbish came into his own by winning the state championship [Michigan Amateur] in 1935, but lost in the finals of that tournament again the last two years.

"Babbish credits Clarence Gamber, Beverly Hills Golf Club professional [while Bob was a member there in 1934], with giving him a number of pointers that have enabled him to improve his game quite a lot in the last year or two."

Then the article goes on to quote Clarence Gamber as saying, "Babbish's game is quite sound all the way around. He has become a very good mashie niblic player, discarding his dynamiter for those short chips around the greens because you can't finesse it with the heavy club. He is studious and he works hard at improving his game. But the greatest improvement I think he has made is in his golfing temperament. He used to become angry or disgusted after a bad shot. Now he has learned to control himself, concentrate his every effort on his next shot. And speaking of shots, he has learned how to do a "punch" iron shot, a trick I taught him, and now he can better me at it."

Some newspaper photographs of Bob taken around this time showing him in various golf swing poses.

Speaking of temperament, when I caddied or played with Bob, he had regained that bad temper when he missed a shot. He was hardest on himself and his worse critic. He never got mad at anyone else, just himself for making a "stupid mistake." As to his "punch" iron shots, he was still playing these well until he stopped playing golf. It was his way out of a bad lie like in the trees. To make a punch iron shot, Bob would take a low-numbered iron to keep the shot low (to avoid the tree limbs) and not follow-through after he hit the ball, instead stopping the swing as soon after making contact with the ball as possible. He usually didn't want to hit the ball too far this way, just to get the ball back into a lie that he could make his next shot from. He taught me how to do it too. Bob was at his best when in a bad situation. I used to tell him it was because he had to think about his shot some more, rather than just use his natural talents to hit the ball.

The 1938 Western Amateur Golf Championship was held at the Chain O' Lakes Country Club in South Bend, Indiana. This was another one of those great tournaments that Bob was fortunate to be able to play in. Originally scheduled to defend his title at the Michigan Open-Amateur that summer, the date for it conflicted with the date for the Western Amateur. Bob probably figured that with the way he was playing that year he had a chance at the Western Amateur. He was a surprise late entry to it.

Because he was given little chance to win it, none of the Detroit newspapers seemed to have sent journalists to cover it even though The Great Babbish and other Michigan golfers, notably Chuck Kocsis and Tommy Sheehan (who played for local South Bend school, Notre Dame, in college) were playing in it. The Detroit golf journalists were instead all covering the Michigan Golf Association Open-Amateur that same weekend.

There were many great amateur golfers from around the country playing and the national press was there covering it. Unlike most of the early golf tournaments Bob played in, many photographs were taken and published of him playing in this event, a few of which are on the following pages.

As you probably know or guessed, Bob won the 1938 Western Amateur Championship. The rest of this chapter will reproduce all that we know of that tournament and Bob's playing in it. This was the high point of his golf career and Bob was proud of winning the Western Amateur his whole life.

A newspaper article dated July 18, 1938 described the finish of the tournament. It stated that the 23-year-old University of Detroit student won the Western Amateur golf championship "after staging a magnificent rally to defeat the seasoned Maurice McCarthy from Cincinnati one-up in their 36-hole final on Sunday." The article went on to say, "Babbish, a smiling brown-haired youngster, achieved the first major victory of his career in conquering McCarthy, an amateur of renown for the last 10 years. McCarthy, former Walker Cup star and National Collegiate champion, predicted that the Detroit youngster would go places in golf. He said Babbish possessed rare talent and a splendid temperament for the game.

"The victory of Babbish was a triumph for youth and stamina over age and experience. The Detroiter, who plays 27 to 36 holes of golf daily, had the stuff at the end to overcome the pressure, which had been upon him for almost six-hours of play. McCarthy, who is 31, showed no signs of weakening until he came to the thirty-fourth hole where he missed a two-foot putt for par. This apparently unnerved the veteran and he drove a tee shot on the thirty-fifth hole into the water, whereas Babbish was on the green and 10 feet from the pin. McCarthy's chip rolled six feet past the cup and he conceded, making Babbish one-up. It was the first time that Babbish had been ahead since the

Bob practicing his chip shot before the final round at the
Western Amateur at Chain O' Lakes Country Club in
South Bend, Indiana in 1938.

Maurice McCarthy, left, shaking hands with Bob, right,
before playing the final rounds at the 1938 Western
Amateur in a wire photograph.

ninth hole of the first 18 played in the morning. It looked
for a moment as if he might lose his advantage because he
sliced into a clump of trees on the final hole, while
McCarthy hit a powerful tee shot down the edge of the
fairway. Babbish played out safely and then hit the shot of
the day, a long iron to the edge of the green.

"McCarthy was square with him, chipping up to within
five feet. Babbish's long putt rolled two feet past the cup
while McCarthy's rolled over. Babbish then sank his for
the victory."

Bob lining up then stroking his winning putt on the last green of the 1938 Western Amateur Championship at Chain O' Lakes Country Club in South Bend, Indiana.

The handshake from opponent McCarthy after Bob won the Western Amateur Golf Championship in 1938

It was hard to believe. The lanky, 23-year-old coal miner's son from humble beginnings wins the golf tournament of every amateur golfer's dream, the Western Amateur. He wasn't supposed to even play in it. He wasn't expected to do well against the national competition. Lord knows how he got the money to even play in it. Bob did the impossible that day and did it in classic Babbish style, coming from behind and winning it on the last hole. Bob truly became The Great Babbish that day. He spoke about it the rest of his life as his greatest golfing achievement. The medal he received for winning the tournament sat on his table, suspended in a Lucite block, until the day he died.

Bob Babbish accepting the Western Amateur Trophy and giving his winner's speech on July 17, 1938.

In an article written two weeks afterwards by E. L. Warner, Jr. entitled "Babbish's Title Takes Rank as Top Amateur Golf Honor," the enormity of this title was emphasized by it starting out saying, "Bob Babbish ran his finger down the long list of names engraved on the big silver George R. Thorne Trophy he was holding. Oldest was that of David R. Forgan, member of an old Chicago golfing family. The year 1899 followed his name. Then came numerous other links notables down to the place where *Robert N. Babbish* was engraved.

"For Babbish has joined the golf elite by his victory in the Western Amateur championship. It is the most important tournament ever won by a Detroit amateur golfer. The field is stronger than the Intercollegiate Championship because it is not restricted to collegians. Virtually the whole country outside of the east and south was represented this year."

The article talked about Bob's improved putting, which Bob attributed to Mortie Dutra and Faust Bianco of the Country Club of Detroit who set him straight. It even said that, "Babbish used an old wood-shafted putter belonging to his sister Rose at South Bend. Someone from an earlier tournament borrowed his putter and failed to return it. His sister's club proved a fine substitute."

Lastly, the article listed Bob's golf schedule for the rest of the season. I have mentioned that he played in tournaments all over the country and this listed two of these lesser known ones that kept Bob busy on the links: Meadowbrook Golf Club four-ball invitational in Northville, Michigan and the Syracuse Yacht Club Invitational in New York.

Bob came back home to Detroit the next day a conquering hero for winning the Western Amateur. He was the first person from Michigan to do so, an honor that still holds true today in 2015. University of Detroit really reaped the praises on him. In another follow-up Western Amateur article (didn't I tell you that none of the Detroit papers were in South Bend when he won and now they had to play catch up?), it said that U of D awarded Bob the major letter "D" for his outstanding work with the golf team including his Western Amateur victory. He was one

## Champion Gets His Trophy

—By News Staff Photographer

Bob Babbish, the Western Amateur Trophy and his big "D."

of the few "minor-sports" stars ever so honored by the Titans. " 'Boy, I will do some tall struttin' with that letter on campus this fall. I will tell them I got it in football' said the sophomore who scored a flock of touchdowns in the golfing world with all his fine play that year."

The article went on to say that Bob "was in the office of Gus Dorais, U of D athletic director, having stopped by to show him the George R. Thorne Trophy he gained possession of through his victory in the Western Amateur. It is one of the oldest trophies in competition, bearing the names of the winners since the inauguration of the tournament in 1899."

Bob's home course, Brooklands Golf and Country Club, had a members' event that August 20th to honor Bob on his victory. After all, some of the glow of victory reflected on his club. Below and on the next pages is the brochure that the Club put together for Bob Babbish Day.

### BROOKLANDS GOLF AND COUNTRY CLUB
*is pleased to announce "BOB BABBISH DAY" Saturday, August 20, 1938, in his honor as the new*
*WESTERN AMATEUR GOLF CHAMPION*

## Activities for the Day

| ENTERTAINMENT *for the* LADIES | ENTERTAINMENT *for the* MEN |
|---|---|
| Buffet Luncheon....................12 to 2 P. M. | Buffet Luncheon....................12 to 2 P. M. |
| Bridge..............................2:00 P. M. | Golf.................................. All Day |
| Individual Table Prizes • Door Prizes | Golf Prizes • Door Prizes |

## Dinner at Eight

Dancing in the evening for all from Nine to One. All
Door and Golf Prizes will be distributed during dinner

Celebrities of athletic sports will be present to help pay homage to a new champion. Bob Babbish will participate in an exhibition match with outstanding players in the Detroit District. We believe this Gala Day will make history at "Brooklands" as the outstanding social event of the year.

Tickets are available at $3.80 per person covering entire day's activities.

Your co-operation in securing tickets for yourselves and guests and making table reservations early will be of great assistance.

ENTERTAINMENT *and* GOLF COMMITTEE

# BROOKLANDS HONORS

## BOB BABBISH
### AUGUST 20, 1938

# WESTERN AMATEUR GOLF CHAMPIONSHIPS
## The Cup, and Its Winners

1899—David R. Forgan
Onwentsia Club

1900—William Waller
Onwentsia Club

1901—Phelps B. Hoyt
Glen View Club

1902—H. Chandler Egan
Exmoor Country Club

1903—Walter E. Egan
Exmoor Country Club

1904—H. Chandler Egan
Exmoor Country Club

1905—H. Chandler Egan
Exmoor Country Club

1906—D. Edwards Sawyer
Wheaton Golf Club

1907—H. Chandler Egan
Exmoor Country Club

1908—Mason E. Phelps
Midlothian Country Club

1909—Charles Evans, Jr.
Edgewater Golf Club

1910—Mason E. Phelps
Midlothian Country Club

1911—Albert Seckel
Riverside Golf Club

1912—Charles Evans, Jr.
Edgewater Golf Club

1913—Warren K. Wood
Homewood Country Club

1914—Charles Evans, Jr.
Edgewater Golf Club

1915—Charles Evans, Jr.
Edgewater Golf Club

1916—Henrich Schmidt
Claremont Country Club

1917—Francis Ouimet
Woodland Golf Club

1919—Harry G. Legg
Minnikahda Club

1920—Charles Evans, Jr.
Edgewater Golf Club

1921—Charles Evans, Jr.
Edgewater Golf Club

1922—Charles Evans, Jr.
Edgewater Golf Club

1923—Charles Evans, Jr.
Edgewater Golf Club

1924—Harrison R. Johnston
White Bear Golf and Country Club

1925—Keefe Carter
Lakeside Golf and Country Club

1926—Frank Dolp
Alderwood Country Club

1927—"Bon" Stein
Seattle Golf Club

1928—Frank Dolp
Alderwood Country Club

1929—Don Moe
Alderwood Country Club

1930—John Lehman
Olympia Fields Country Club

1931—Don Moe
Aldfwood Country Club

1932—Gus Moreland
Dallas Country Club

1933—Jack Westland
Sun Set Ridge

1934—Zell Eaton
Edgemere Golf and Country Club

1935—Charles R. Yates
Atlanta Athletic Club

1936—Paul Leslie
Jefferson City, Missouri

1937—Wilford Wehrle
Racine Country Club

## 1938 — "Bob" Babbish
### Brooklands Golf & Country Club

In the afterglow of Bob's Western Amateur victory there was one last article dated August 19, 1938 that was not so much about Bob but about a friend of his that supported him at the tournament.

The article explained that, "Bud Stillman was one of Bob's biggest fans at the time. He was a member of Brooklands and happened to be in South Bend on business the day of the first round of the Western Amateur. Bud followed Bob as he pulled the first two close matches out of the fire. Bud was expected to be in Detroit that evening as his wife had a birthday party planned for him that day. But that evening Bud telephoned his wife saying 'I just helped Bob pull through two close matches today and I want to get him started off right tomorrow then I will be right home.' So the party was postponed one night." Below is Bob and Bud in South Bend at the tournament.

"Bob had two more close calls playing the second day and again Bud called his wife: 'I can't leave him now – I'll be home tomorrow for sure.'

"Bob won two more exciting matches on Saturday, putting him into the finals. Bud didn't telephone his wife that night, he wired her, 'A little strategy any husband can appreciate' to avoid actually talking to her. Party canceled a third time.

"The next morning Babbish received a wire from Mrs. Stillman, explaining her dilemma. After Bob marched to victory in the finals with Stillman at his side now the whole tournament, he speedily dispatched him home. Stillman reached home just before the thrice-postponed party broke up."

The article went on to say that Bud was instrumental in arranging The Bob Babbish Day at Brooklands and he made sure that it wasn't the usual "stag" affair but that women were also invited to attend.

With all of Bob's success on the links in 1938 there was a strong rumor that he was being considered to play on the U.S. team in the 1940 Walker Cup Match. The Walker Cup is the name of the trophy received when a team wins the Walker Cup Match and it pits a hand-selected team from the United States against one from Great Britain and Ireland. It was played every other year and its all-amateur players from the U.S. were picked by the United States Golf Association. There was a photograph of Bob holding the Western Amateur George R. Thorne Trophy with the caption "Trophy May Lead to Walker Cup" published in a Detroit paper around this time. Another article said Bob was "material" for the 1940 Walker Cup team.

Sadly because of World War II the Walker Cup Match was canceled that year through 1946 and Bob never did play in it, a disappointment he carried to his death.

# CHAPTER 5
## BIG MAN ON CAMPUS: 1936 TO 1940

After being a "golf bum" for three years after graduating from high school, Bob enrolled at the University of Detroit for college in the fall of 1936. U of D was the Jesuit Catholic college in Detroit and had a great sports reputation, especially in football. It was located off of McNichols Road on the near west side of town, about six miles from Bob's home on Moenart Street.

Bob was the first Babbish to attend college, a point of great pride for Anna and the rest of the family. Being a private school, the tuition was higher than nearby Wayne State University, the huge public college in Detroit, but it made no difference as golf was paying off again, this time in the form of a scholarship for Bob.

Being from a poor family, the only way Bob could afford to attend college was with a scholarship. And the University of Detroit offered him one for golf. It worked out great for both parties: Bob got to go to college and U of D got a good Polish Catholic kid, not to mention one that could play some golf! He was a member of the golf team his first year in college in 1936 and remained on it for all four years he attended U of D. While in college, in 1938 Bob was ranked the Number 1 collegiate golfer in Michigan and was also ranked the fourth best amateur in the United States by Grantland Rice, the famous sportswriter and radio personality. Bob always looked back at his years at U of D as being the best of his life. The pride of attending college, the first in his family ever to do so, doing well in his studies and, because of his golf, being the "big man on campus," lasted his whole life.

U of D's landmark Clock Tower in 2015, pretty much the same as when Bob attended school there in the late 1930's.

When he started playing for the U of D golf team in the 1936/37 school year, Bob was immediately named the captain of the golf team. Not only was he playing in college tournaments for his school, he was also playing in all the other golf tournaments that we have been reading about in the prior chapter and continued to do so through college in his own name (with U of D enjoying the resulting positive publicity).

Above is the 1937/38 U of D golf team, the second year Bob played on it. He is the second from the left. The names of the other players are lost to memory. U of D took a lot of publicity photographs of their golf team and the local Detroit press often published them. Many of the photographs of Bob's college days in this book were taken from newspapers though he did have original prints of some of them in his files.

The long-time U of D golf coach those years was Professor William Kelly Joyce. When I once asked what Professor Joyce taught at U of D, Bob couldn't recall him ever teaching anything. That was because Prof. Joyce taught at U of D School of Law, which was located on a different campus downtown. Prof. Joyce was also a frequent host of U of D's radio show "Ask the Professor" (which is still broadcast) and even acted as a judge on the original television courtroom show "Traffic Court" which

Above is a photograph of the golf coach William Kelly Joyce on the "Ask the Professor" radio show broadcast out of U of D in the early 1940's.

was broadcast on a local Detroit TV station for years. I remember watching it as a kid and Bob telling me that the judge was his golf coach. Boy, I really felt sorry for Dad to have a judge as a coach.

The 1938/39 U of D Golf Team is seen above with Bob second from right and the names of the others lost to time.

Bob was enrolled in the School of Commerce and Finance, "C&F" for short, and his major there was in Foreign Trade. This was a preview of what Bob had in mind for his future. As we know, he never became a professional golfer (he probably would have been one by then and never attended college) but had planned to continue to play golf as an amateur and have it supplement a business career for him. At this early age Bob had figured

Pictures of the Commerce & Finance Building in 2015.

out that as a businessman, especially in sales, his company would encourage him to continue his golfing success as it would reflect on the company and could be used as a magnet to garner business. Many businessmen were becoming golfers back then and all of them from Michigan wanted to play with The Great Babbish. Bob was able to use this to mix golf and work until he retired and also have his company pay for a club membership, green fees and other golf, er, I mean business, expenses. Bob was one smart guy. No wonder he was the first Babbish to attend college. Got it from Anna his mother.

A photograph of Coach William Kelly Joyce and Bob at U of D that was autographed by Coach Joyce: "To 'My Bob' with best wishes for future accomplishments."

Bob was Coach Joyce's favorite golfer of all time at U of D. This was because Bob was the greatest golfer the U of D golf team had and has ever seen. There were a number of articles in the Detroit papers at this time and later about Coach Joyce's admiration for Bob. One such article published while Bob was in World War II said, "No one can talk about golf with Prof. Joyce without him referring to 'my boy, Bob.' 'Bob's more than a great golfer,' Prof. Joyce always says, 'He's a real sportsman and a credit to the game.' All who knew the former District and Western Amateur champion will agree with U of D's coach." Below is a photograph that was taken of Coach Joyce in his office on campus with golf photographs from his scrapbook, including many of Bob.

TITAN COACH AND HIS WARRIORS OF THE LINKS

With CAPT. BOB BABBISH showing the way, University of Detroit's golf team yesterday defeated Michigan Normal at Red Run. Left to right are: AUGIE FOG- OROS, JACK DAVIDSON, COACH WILLIAM KELLY JOYCE, HENRY BRODIE and BABBISH. The Titans have broken even in four games played thus far.

Above is the 1939/40 U of D Golf Team in a newspaper clipping with Bob on the far right and Coach Joyce in the center. Another publicity shot appears on the following page. This was Bob's last year playing on the team before graduating from college.

When Bob played at U of D they won 37 tournaments. Bob won 24 out of 27 individual matches during his four years and had a 73.1 stroke average. As mentioned, he did all this while playing in many non-collegiate golf events at the same time as well as working on his college degree in Foreign Trade.

Bob was also working during the summers while at school. One summer he was hired as a welder at the Dodge Main plant in nearby Hamtramck. He said it was the only job he had that he could have been killed doing it, as it was so dangerous. He only lasted a short time working there before quitting. The next summer he worked at the Plymouth car plant on Lynch Road in Detroit that was closer to his home on Moenart Street as a timekeeper's assistant, a much safer job according to Bob.

## Winter's Return Doesn't Blight U. D. Golf Hopes

JACK DAVIDSON    STEVE BRODIE    BOB BABBISH    AUGIE FOGOROS

Two veterans and two sophomores comprise the University of Detroit golf team which opens the season today, playing Purdue at Lafayette, Ind.—of course, if weather permits. The veterans are Capt. Bob Babbish and Augie Fogoros, seniors. Newcomers are Jack Davidson and Steve Brodie. All four are Detroiters. So is the present alternate on the team, Charles Gamber, sophomore, a brother of Clarence Gamber. Besides Purdue, the Titans play three other Big Ten schools, Illinois, Northwestern and Indiana.

During his last summer at U of D in 1940, Bob was hired as a gardener at the farmland that Henry Ford maintained in Dearborn, Michigan, home to his huge auto manufacturing complex (Ford did this for getting a tax break on his vacant land). Every summer Ford hired a lot of college students to work the land and pick the crops. Bob told the story that one of the work rules there was that, "Employees cannot, repeat, cannot eat the crops while working by order of Mr. Ford himself."

Bob, being a "Depression Baby," had developed a fondness for some simple foods. He loved an onion sandwich (in later years the Detroit Golf Club even offered one on their lunch menu and named it "The Babbish") and eating tomatoes like apples.

Well, you can guess the rest of the story. Bob was picking tomatoes of all things one day while working the Ford gardens and couldn't resist eating one right there on the spot. Before he was done with it he was grabbed from behind by the collar by no other than Mr. Ford himself, who was inspecting the gardeners at the time, and was promptly fired on the spot by The Man. Bob spent the rest of that summer working at the family gas station. I once related this story to Ford's great grandson Edsel who replied that that was the Henry Ford he knew!

Looking through old copies of U of D yearbooks, I found out a fair amount of information not only about the golf team but also about Bob's college years.

The U of D Titan Yearbook for 1937 noted that Bob played in the interschool Fisher Golf Tournament on October 1, a tournament open to all U of D students. Bob won it with a 72-77 for 36 holes. U of D's golf season that year saw them beat Western State Teachers College (now Western Michigan University) 18-9 in the rain, University of Toledo 12-6, Armour Tech of Chicago 13-5 and

Michigan State Normal Teacher's College (now Eastern Michigan University).

During the 1937/38 season they played Purdue and University of Indiana right off and lost both. Then they played Notre Dame and made history by defeating the Irish for the first time in any sport at U of D. Bob led his teammates with rounds of 77 and 74 over the long Oakland Hills, Michigan course to take three points from Notre Dame captain and Indiana Intercollegiate champion, Tommy Sheehan, another Detroit boy and a good friend.

In an article written by E. A. Batchelor, Jr. about the victory over Notre Dame that the photograph on the next page was published with, the emphasis was on Notre Dame sophomore Walter Hagen, Jr., son of the famous and flamboyant golfer Walter Hagen. It said the Walter Jr. played a tremendous first round at Oakland Hills that day with a 74 but slumped in the afternoon round with an 81. The article said that Hagen was not surprised by the poor round as, "He had been told by no less an authority than his father that he would never make a golfer. The elder Hagen had dissuaded him from playing golf until four years ago, declaring his son not serious minded enough for top-flight competition. Until recently the young Hagen had proved his father an excellent prophet. The senior Hagen, now on a world tour, does not know his son has made the Notre Dame team. 'He'll go out like a light when I tell him about the 74,' young Haig said."

The article then went on to say, "Bob Babbish, one of the three sophomores on Detroit's team, turned in the most consistent golf. Babbish scored a 77 in the morning and, teamed with Bob Dilworth, split three points with the Notre Dame pair of Tom Sheehan and Bob Gallagher. In the afternoon, Babbish, holder of the state open amateur title, scored a 74, sweeping three points from Sheehan.

## First U. of D. Team to Beat Notre Dame

University of Detroit's golf team is the first Titan sports squad to beat Notre Dame. The feat was accomplished Monday at Oakland Hills. Members of the team, left to right, are: Bob Dilworth, Augie Fogoros, Mark Walsh, Bob Babbish, Carl Collett and Bob Temple.

Babbish was aided by a brilliant second nine, coming back in 35."

Later that same 1937/38 season the Titans lost to Northwestern and then came back to beat Toledo, Michigan Normal and Western State Teacher College (now Eastern Michigan University and Western Michigan University, respectively) with Bob being the low medalist in those last two matches with a 72 and 74, respectively.

The 1938/39 school year started with Bob winning the William Kelly Joyce Trophy in the intramural golf tournament from a field of 29. The golf team had its toughest schedule in its history that year, which included matches with five Big 10 Conference colleges including Northwestern (U of D lost but the featured match was Bob playing two-time Western Conference champion Syd Richardson and defeating him 73 to 76), University of Illinois (lost), Michigan State Normal Teachers College (now Eastern Michigan University, won), Purdue (lost), Indiana University (lost), Ohio State (won, the U of D team playing their best ever and Bob shooting a one under par 71), and Western State Teachers College (now Western Michigan University, tie, with Bob registering his seventh straight victory in match play that season).

Bob's biggest intercollegiate game was also his last one. It was at the end of the 1939/40 season and was against Notre Dame. As you can see from the newspaper clipping on the next page, there was local coverage of this event as it was always a big deal when these two Catholic colleges played each other in any sport back then. What made it special was not only was it Bob's last college game but also that the captain of the Notre Dame team was now Walter Hagen, Jr. Though Team U of D lost to Team Notre Dame that game, Bob beat Hagen in the individuals with a 71 at Red Run Golf Club in Royal Oak, the first time a U of D player had ever beaten a Notre Dame one in golf.

In an article in The Detroit News dated May 14, 1940 entitled "24th Victory for Babbish, U of D Golf Captain Whips Young Hagen," journalist John Walter wrote, "Bob Babbish and Walter Hagen, Jr., two young golfers in whom Detroiters are more than ordinarily interested, ended their careers as captains of U of D and Notre Dame golf teams, respectively, at Red Run Saturday. Babbish shot a sub-par

# Irish Makes Notre Dame's

Even the son of the great "Haig" has trap trouble now and then. Here the Notre Dame captain is shown plowing his way out of the sand as, left to right, U. of D.'s BOB BAB- BISH, JACK DAVIDSON and Notre Dame's WILLIAM SCHALLER watch. Babbish, in his final match as a Titan golfer, scored an impressive victory over Hagen.

71 to beat young Hagen, 3 to 2, but Hagen's team won the match.

"After keeping members of both teams waiting an hour on the tee because he overslept, Hagen showed up at Red Run Golf Club at 9:45 am then still had to catch a bite to eat and hit a couple of shots before he joined the impatient members of the rival team to do battle."

Another article commented on this event that, "Like his father, Walter Jr. has a personality that melts away anything before him. Much as they might have liked to, no one could get peeved at him for this antic.

"Hagen came up with a big hole on the ninth to split the point for the first nine with Babbish who was out in 37, one over par, to Hagen's 38. Babbish bagged a pair of birdies on the twelfth and fifteenth holes and was even par the rest of the way to trim Hagen 3-up with 2 to play. A drive out of bounds on Number 15 started Hagen off to three bogies in a row and he wound up with a 77. But he was cheerful and almost totally unconcerned over the results of the match, congratulating Babbish with a sincerity and enthusiasm that would cause an outsider to wonder that he had lost.

"In that respect, Hagen was just like his Dad. 'Every day he grows more like his Dad, The Haig,' Mortie Dutra, the Red Run professional remarked as Hagen, Jr. came gliding over the hill on the last hole. The characteristic Hagen pose, with hands on hips, as he studied a lie in the rough, his mannerism as he addressed the ball, his fast backswing, all were points Dutra mentioned as being identical with The Haig's."

Fast forwarding a bit since we are talking about Bob's college days: In December 1951, The Detroit News asked the public relations department of Wayne State University, Michigan State University, University of Detroit and the University of Michigan to select their 10 most distinguished athletes. At that time there was no collegiate Hall of Fame in Michigan to do this. In the article about the U of D all-time rankings, their hand-selected ten most distinguished athletes included Bob in the honor, one of two golfers. Five were football players, one baseball and one basketball.

BABBISH

An undated shot of Bob hitting balls while at U of D.

The title of this 1940 U of D publicity photo says it all.

As mentioned, Bob was still playing in other golf tournaments while at college. He was the runner up in the Michigan Open to Marvin Stahl by one stroke at the Western Golf and Country Club in nearby Redford, MI in 1939.

Also in 1939 he again qualified for the U.S. Open Championship, one of ten local Detroit golfers to do so, and played in it at the Philadelphia Country Club in Gladwyne, PA. Byron Nelson won it that year, his first and only time. There is no record on how well Bob played there that year.

Well, 1939 didn't turn out to be as good a golf season as the rest of that decade had been for Bob. Sure he was playing for the U of D golf team and was going to college. Plus he was still living at home and had to work to contribute to Babbish Enterprises, usually at the garage he owned with brothers Frank and Walter. Bob was starting to feel some pressure to keep up the pace of The Great Babbish.

Local writer George Maskin picked up on this and wrote an article dated June 29, 1940 about a tip Bob received from a friend about his physical fitness, or lack thereof, in 1939. "The friend interceded in Babbish's behalf midway during the 1938/39 season. Babbish was having a tough time on the links. In fact, he had troubles all year, failing to win any kind of championship for the first time in four or five campaigns.

"Babbish fretted over his difficulties, as any star would. He began to visualize funny things, including the fact his golf game was on the verge of collapse. At this state, the friend in waiting rushed in with the wise word. He suggested, and he used Babbish himself as the model, that Bob go on a diet, get rid of the excess fat on his body and stop being so sluggish. The tip only drew a sneer from

Babbish, however, when first presented. Babbish knew differently. 'Where do you get that stuff on me being fat and sluggish?' Babbish popped back at the friend. 'I weigh 185 pounds, and there's nothing wrong in that figure, considering I am 24 years old.' But persistence didn't help Babbish's golf. Titles continued to elude him, through faulty performances here and there along the line. Action, Babbish deemed, was necessary.

?ORTS      Monday, February 12, 1940

**GIRDS FOR GOLF SEASON**

Bob Babbish, one of Detroit's leading golfers, keeps in trim for the 1940 season by playing handball. Babbish formerly held the Western and State Amateur titles and was runnerup to Marvin Stahl for the State Open crown last Summer.

Handball was a big part of Bob's 1939/40 exercise routine.

"He finally accepted the good words of the friend. It was too late to do anything about 1939. Like the football coach, he commenced preparing for the next season. During the winter, Babbish lost 15 pounds. He started the 1940 golf season tipping the beams at 170. Besides, he confesses the sluggishness which hindered him a year ago now has disappeared completely."

We already know how well Bob played for U of D in the 1939/40 golf season, which began in April that year, his last year on the team as it was his year to graduate. Well, getting physically fit over that winter also brought its rewards on the non-collegiate golf circuit.

In 1940 Bob qualified again for the U.S. Open for a third time in a row. It was held at Canterbury Golf Club in Beachwood, Ohio just outside of Cleveland. In the sectional qualifying he shared low amateur honors with fellow Detroiter (and now Notre Dame graduate) Tommy Sheehan. That year Lawson Little won and Bob made a "credible showing" finishing 52nd overall with a 309 total score, what turned out to be his best U.S. Open performance in the seven times he played in it.

Bob was scheduled to travel to Manchester, Vermont to play in the National Intercollegiate Tournament in June 1940. But at the last moment he canceled the trip at the insistence of U of D athletic director Gus Dorais and Golf Coach William Kelly Joyce. This was a tough decision for him to make, as it was his last chance to play in this national tournament as he was graduating from college that year. And that was the problem. Bob had accepted a job with a tire company in Ohio starting in August but under the condition that he had his college degree first. In order to finish his degree he had to go to summer school. Going to Vermont would have meant missing the first week of the short, condensed summer semester at U of D.

Bob seriously thought of going against the advice of Dorais and Joyce but their wisdom prevailed and Bob sadly withdrew his name from the tournament. He had set his heart on playing this tournament that year and was a favorite to win it, making a credible showing at the U.S. Open in Cleveland two weeks before. In an article about this Bob is quoted as saying "I know that I've done the wisest thing, but gosh, I sure would like a last crack at that title!" Bob was always the competitor, wasn't he?

Funny how things worked out as Bob instead played in the local 1940 Detroit District Golf Association District Championship on June 23rd, one that wouldn't interfere too much with summer school classes, and won it for the first time. "Bob Babbish, the smiling, black-haired crusader of the links, today is king of the district's golfers" read the first line of Bob Murphy's article on the 1940 Detroit District Championship in the Detroit Free Press. He slushed through 13 holes in the rain to beat the cool and always dangerous Chris Brinke, Oakland Hills veteran, 6 and 5. Three times before – in 1935, 1936 and 1937 – Babbish had gone as far as the semifinals in district title play. It was the same Brinke who beat him his first year out over the same course where he conquered Chris yesterday. The next year Walter Gow eliminated him at Essex Country Club across the Detroit River in Ontario. Francis Ryan handed him his next disappointment in the semifinals in 1937.

"In his fourth quest for the title, Babbish had the shots, the poise and the important putting touch to win. Like the wind and the rain, he was very much in Brinke's hair all the way. Babbish had a 34, one under par, for the first nine and when the match ended on the thirteenth he was still one under par. Considering the weather conditions, this was championship golf of the first degree."

Another article about the 1940 District tournament by Mark Beltaire for The Detroit News added, "It was an especially welcome victory for Babbish who hadn't won a tournament since he captured the Western Amateur championship in 1938 and it may be his farewell to golf in Michigan for at least a bit. Bob, who represents Brooklands Golf and Country Club, thinks he may skip the state [amateur] championship at Charlevoix in July and when summer school ends in August he expects to go to work for a rubber company in Hartsville, Ohio near Canton."

Another piece of information about Bob while he was attending U of D was that he was very active in the intramural sports there, even being on the intramural sports committee his last year in college.

The intramural sports he played included handball, which as we know Bob enjoyed playing. When I was attending high school we had a couple of handball courts out behind the school and a number of students used to play it. One day Bob was dropping me off at school and noticed them. He casually mentioned to me that he played handball when he was young. I was surprised as I did not connect it with him. When I pressed him on it he said it was a sport from the Great Depression: "All you needed was a ball and a wall."

He was also written up twice in the Titans yearbook over the years about taking time out of his busy golf, study and work schedule to teach co-eds the finer points of the game of golf. On the next page is a photo that was published showing fifteen young women with golf clubs all taking a moment to look at the camera instead of at Bob instructing them on the far right of the shot. Tough job but someone had to teach them. He was also in the Delta Phi Epsilon fraternity for majors in Foreign Trade.

Bob was very proud of attending U of D and always considered himself an "educated" man because of it, something that not many people could say at that time. In many ways it was remarkable that Bob was able to do it and all the other things he did during that period of his life.

When you walk around U of D today, now named University of Detroit Mercy, most of the campus looks the same as when Bob attended there. This can be seen in the photographs appearing earlier this chapter of the Commerce & Finance building taken in 2015, eighty years later. The campus was just ten years old when Bob arrived there in 1936, being built during the golden age of Detroit that started in the 1920's.

Above is Bob, his wife Delphine and the author at my graduation from U of D in 1972 where we were posing in front of the sports display that contained photographs of Bob when he was playing golf at U of D. This was before the U of D Titan Hall of Fame was initiated.

Eventually, in 1977, the University of Detroit did create an athlete hall of fame. Called the Detroit Titans Hall of Fame, Bob was inducted to it in 1980. At Calihan Hall, the indoor sports complex on campus, is a wall honoring Bob and all his achievements. On the previous page is a shot of the wall there with Bob's section and below is his plaque.

**UNIVERSITY OF DETROIT**
Sports Hall of Fame

*In recognition of outstanding achievement and contribution to University of Detroit athletics*

## BOB BABBISH

Golf, 1936-38
No. 1 collegiate golfer in nation in 1938
Won 1938 Western Open title and 1935 Michigan Amateur championship

*has been inducted into the*
*U-D Sports Hall of Fame*
**1980**

Bob did graduate in August 1940, as planned, with his business degree. He had that job in the tire industry all lined up right after he graduated. And, as he had planned, his college degree eventually gave him a very good life, one where he made sufficient money to raise a family and send them to college and also play his golf as part of his job as a salesman for various companies over the years. A playing out of the American Dream for a coal miner's son from Pennsylvania. I have often wondered what Bob's life would have been like if, instead of going to college, he had turned professional like so many of his golfing friends did back then? Certainly it would have been a far different life for him. But Bob's life, as millions others, hit a brick wall in 1940's as World War II stepped in and changed his plans.

Two more U of D publicity photographs of Bob taken in 1940 on this page and the prior one. They were probably taken at the nearby Detroit public golf course at Palmer Park, located just a couple miles from U of D, where the golf team practiced at that time.

# CHAPTER 6
## YOU'RE IN THE ARMY NOW: 1940 TO 1945

For Bob, World War II was the worst of times and the best of times. As to the worst of times, though he never said anything about them I heard from others that Bob came back pretty "shell-shocked" as they called it back then. After returning from the War, Bob moved in with his brother John, his wife Esther and their new, young family on Collingham Street on Detroit's far east side (known as "Copper Corridor" as so many police and firemen lived in the area). John told me on a number of occasions that Bob was pretty shaken up by the War and that he took some time to recover. He would know as he probably nursed Bob back to health, being the big brother John was.

As to the best of times, Bob got to see Europe, courtesy of Uncle Sam. When Bob did talk about his war years it was always about something non-war-like, like how beautiful Paris was, or London's city life, or the Rhine River; a tourist's story of a trip instead of that of a soldier of war. Bob said that at one point he seriously thought of making a career out of the Army as there was a U.S. General encouraging him to do so.

Bob technically joined the Army right out of college in September 1940 when he joined the Michigan National Guard. His first tour of duty was in 1941 and he took a troop train to Seattle, WA to join the 126th Coastal Infantry there. In late 1941 he went to officer training school and was commissioned as a second lieutenant in the quarter master corps assigned to the 29th Artillery Division. He did maneuvers throughout the southern United States until 1942 when he was shipped out to Salisbury, England. He was in England for two years until D-Day in 1944 and landed in France ten days later by landing craft and did quartermaster duty for the 29th Artillery Division there. Later in 1944 Bob was transferred to the 13th Corps Special forces as a Special Services Officer where he, among other things, handled distributing rationed goods to the soldiers, escorting celebrities who entertained the troops and arranging for intercompany sports activities throughout France and Germany until the end of the War.

BOB BABBISH        JACK McDERMOTT        CHAS. GANSTER        JIM ELLIS

Bob once told me the story of his enlisting in the Army. He said that you had a choice of being drafted or joining voluntarily and that you were better off joining. Apparently the draft that year reached him so he and a few of his U of D classmates joined in 1940. These included

Jim "Zip" Ellis, Jack McDermott, Charles Ganster and Bob Gajda, some seen in the photograph on the prior page with Bob in their uniforms right after boot camp. Two of these volunteers, Jim Ellis and Bob Gajda, were golfing friends of Bob, with Gajda becoming a professional golfer after the War (one summer in high school I worked in Gajda's rack room and pro shop at Forest Lake Country Club in Bloomfield Hills as Bob got me the job through this friendship). Ellis later became an Oldsmobile dealer.

As Bob was a local sports star, the Detroit newspapers covered his departure for the Army in a number of articles, all with a golf angle. Below are some of these articles along with some photographs on this theme that were published in the Detroit Times. The one article said that Bob was stationed with the 210th Coast Artillery at Fort Sheridan, Illinois then and some Detroit friends of the popular young golf star predicted that he was going to make a splendid soldier because as "a thorough-going youngster he has succeeded in everything he has tackled."

Another article was lamenting the fact that the War and draft would make the picking of contenders in the local golf tournaments difficult that year, and that "the major events involving the mighty males will be wide open." It went on to say under the sub-title "Will Miss Babbish" that "the Detroit District Golf Association, as an example, is certain to have a new champion – unless Uncle Sam should be kind to Bob Babbish and grant him a furlough." There was another newspaper article alluding to the fact that Bob had moved to Ohio for that job with the tire company saying, "Babbish, who has been living in Ohio since his graduation from the University of Detroit, will try his marksmanship in an anti-aircraft unit" and that he was then back at home in Detroit awaiting the summons to join a National Guard unit.

Bob entered the Army as a First Lieutenant, a "first louey" as one article described it in a gossip column telling the Detroit ladies that unmarried Bob was still "available." When Bob went overseas to Salisbury, England in 1942, he was involved in the preparations for D-Day with the 29th Infantry Division. I remember asking him once when I was a kid if he was in D-Day, probably when I first found out about it. He solemnly told me that he was supposed to go over on D-Day and even a day before (D-Day Minus One) to prepare for the invasion at Normandy but a few days beforehand was reassigned. That was all he said but I got the impression that that was a good thing. He did land in France on D-Day + 10. He later confirmed that the soldier who took his place on D-Day survived unharmed. One Detroit newspaper had a short article about Bob and D-Day that took the lighter side of the event, saying that the Army Press headquarters credited Bob with "dashing into the Normandy offensive with rifle in one hand and a mashie-niblick club in the other."

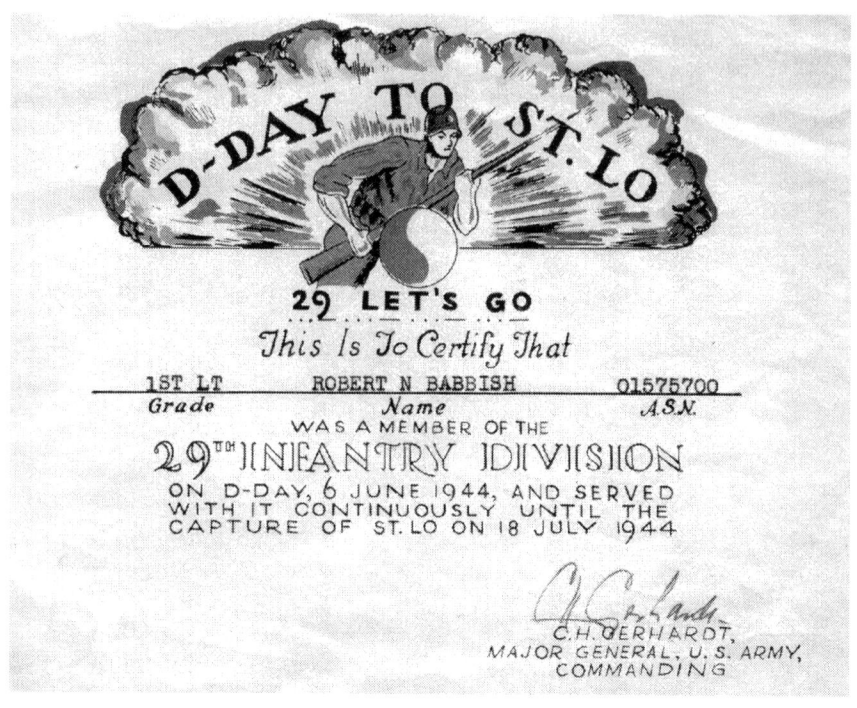

D-DAY TO ST. LO

29 LET'S GO

*This Is To Certify That*

| 1ST LT | ROBERT N BABBISH | 01575700 |
| --- | --- | --- |
| *Grade* | *Name* | *A.S.N.* |

WAS A MEMBER OF THE

29TH INFANTRY DIVISION

ON D-DAY, 6 JUNE 1944, AND SERVED WITH IT CONTINUOUSLY UNTIL THE CAPTURE OF ST. LO ON 18 JULY 1944

C.H. GERHARDT,
MAJOR GENERAL, U. S. ARMY,
COMMANDING

A certificate given to Bob from Major General C. H. Gerhardt regarding D-Day. Saint-Lo was a French town instrumental in securing as part of the Allied invasion.

As mentioned, at some point after D-Day Bob was transferred to another division, this one a bit safer. This was the 13th Corps Special Services Division. This transfer might have been because of Bob's outgoing personality and the way he got along with everyone. He was promoted to a Captain, the rank he retained until he left the Army in 1945.

As Bob said, being in Special Services was a tough job but someone had to do it. Part of his duties there related to the USO and the entertainment of the troops. He met Bob Hope during the many times he went to entertain the troops. He also mentioned meeting Dinah Shore once in

Europe and then running into her again 50 years later on a golf course in Florida and Dinah remembering him from the War. She recalled that Bob let her use his helmet as a bowl to wash her hair in before a performance. Bob was also in charge of rationed goods in Europe during the War including cigarettes, liquor, coffee, etc. so he was a very popular guy.

Capt. Bob in the 13th Corps Special Services during WWII.

Bob in combat fatigues in Holland in 1944.

Captain Bob in dress uniform in Europe during the War.

I have a large envelope of photographs from Bob's
WWII days. The photographs reproduced in this book are
just a sampling of them. One has to presume that Bob took
all the photographs other than those taken of him, which
were taken by friends. On the back of each one is the
stamp of the Army Censor Examiner clearing it (or, in
some instances, not). In a few of the pictures Bob has a
camera around his neck. It must have been part of his job
to take photographs of the War though he was not an
Army photographer as far as I know. The interesting thing
is that I do not remember Bob ever even holding a camera
when I was a kid, least of all taking family photographs.
That was always Mom's job.

A photo that Bob took of the Arc de Triomphe de l'Étoile
in Paris when the Allies liberated Paris in 1945.

Bob in front of barracks somewhere in Europe.

A relaxed Bob reading in a field in Europe during WWII,
rifles and a military vehicle in the background.

A wartime Christmas card from Uncle Bob to his brother John's children, obviously after the liberation of Paris.

An Army-issued Mothers Day Card from Bob to Anna while he was in service in World War II that was saved over the years along with his many War photographs.

Bob did mention to me a few times about meeting General George Patton during the War. From what I recall Bob telling me, the above photograph might be of Patton, in the center with his back toward the camera, General Eisenhower on the left and Field Marshall Bernard Montgomery on the right, three of the leaders of the Allies during WWII, having a street meeting in Holland in 1944.

CAPT. ROBERT N. BABISH
U. S. Army
State Amateur Champion, 1935

A publicity photo taken of Bob donating to a Red Cross campaign during the War that appeared in local papers.

Another War story Bob told me was about the dog he had in London. He said that the Germans were bombing London nightly when he was there and that the dog they had was their own personal air raid siren. Bob swore that that dog could sense the Nazi V-1 flying bombs before they crossed the English Channel and would start whining and barking and would hide underneath the bed. The dog's name was Callie and there she is with Bob in London in the photograph on the next page.

Bob with the air raid siren dog Callie in London during
World War II.

A formal portrait of Captain Robert N. Babbish.

As World War II was winding down, Bob wrote a letter to brother John and his family that somehow survived over the years. It was dated April 15, 1945 and the envelope and each page are shown below and on the following pages. In case you cannot read his handwriting, it talks about President Franklin D. Roosevelt dying just three days earlier on April 12 and wondering what was going to come from it. About the War winding down and Bob hoping it would be over soon as he wanted to go home. He also said that he was looking forward to going back to work when the War was over, and thanks for the package, the shrimp in it was used at a party. He also asked about the family gas station, whether his Army pay was arriving on time and if brother Frank was up to any new business ventures, Frank's business luck having been pretty good so far.

Above is the envelope mailed to Bob's brother and sister-in-law in Detroit postmarked April 17, 1945 from Europe.

Page one of Bob's April 15, 1945 War letter from Europe.

Page two of Bob's April 15, 1945 War letter from Europe.

the money. It shouldn't make any change in your receiving a monthly check as they are to come regular anyway. Let me know please. — Don't forget anytime you need any money. Just take it — Never mind asking. How are the kids? I guess they are looking forward to vacation time — Me too! Only I don't want a vacation — I want a discharge so I can go home — start working and get married — You know I'm going back to work for

Page three of Bob's April 15, 1945 War letter from Europe.

Henry Morris. I don't think I could do better - do you? Anything doing at the Gas Station? Has Frank any lines on some new venture into business? He has been very lucky up to date - Hope he doesn't pick on a bad one - Everything is OK with me as a matter of fact I couldn't be better - Hope this finds you as well - Regards to the gang and please don't worry

As ever
Bob

Page four of Bob's April 15, 1945 War letter from Europe.

As a kid I was very interested in World War II and the military equipment and airplanes in it, same as every kid my age was. Only a few times would Bob allow me to engage him on this topic. Once was when in 1972 Volkswagen came out with their Type 181 car they called the "Thing" to supplement its popular Beetle model. When Bob first saw a VW Thing in Detroit he said that it was the German Army's VW Type 82 personnel carrier, their "Jeep" vehicle, reincarnated like one he drove in the War. Below is a picture Bob took of a VW Type 82 in its original military version in Germany that was captured and used by the Special Services for deliveries. From the can of paint in the foreground it seems like they just repainted it for the U. S. Army.

Another shot of Bob in action in World War II now assigned to the 13th Corps Special Services, which included USO duties and escorting celebrities entertaining the troops in Europe. He is in that VW Type 82 vehicle they captured and we saw on the prior page just after they repainted it for the U.S. Army. Note the convertible top is down now.

Bob in the back of an Army transport vehicle in France.

Bob standing in the back of another Army vehicle, this one
taken in front of a church in Paris in 1944.

Another interesting War story from Bob was prompted by the group of photographs that follow. I came across them one day and asked him about them. Bob said that the destroyed plane in the photographs was the first German jet that was shot down. It was near the end of the War and the Germans put these first-ever jet planes into service earlier than planned out of desperation as they were losing the War then. They didn't work out as the Germans had hoped, which was a good thing for us.

Bob with a shot-down German jet near the end of the War.

Bob leaning on the shot-down German jet fighter plane.

Above is another shot of that downed German jet and below is another captured German fighter plane Bob saw.

In May 1945 the War in Europe was over. In June
1945, Bob was granted furlough to go home to Detroit.
Above is a photograph Bob took of the ship that took him
home while he was waiting to board.

Bob when he had just joined the Army with a nephew and niece on a 1941 Plymouth. Compare this with the shots on the following pages when he came home in 1945.

During a furlough home in July 1945 after the War in Europe had ended, his family gave Bob a large homecoming party in Detroit. Bob had been in the military almost five years now and everyone was eager to see him again. In his letter reproduced earlier Bob mentioned that he just wanted to get home and get a job, get married and start a family, the longing of all the soldiers in World War II. One can understand why this was particularly so as by now Bob had plenty of nieces and nephews from his brothers and sister, most of who were married by now.

Bob with mother Anna during the homecoming celebration thrown for him during his furlough in July 1945 after being away in Europe for three years during World War II.

Another photograph at the welcome home party for Bob in
1945 while he was on furlough. Life had gone on while
Bob was in the Army for five years and he came home to a
whole bunch of nieces and nephews, all who adored,
though maybe never met, their War hero Uncle Bob.

At the end of his furlough in the summer of 1945, Bob
was ordered to board another troop train for Seattle. His
assignment there was to begin training along with other
troops arriving home from the War in Europe for the
invasion of Japan as that war was still going on. As we all

know, this invasion never happened. In August of 1945 the U.S. dropped the atomic bombs on Japan, ending World War II. Once when I was a kid Bob told me that but for the atomic bomb he would have possibly died fighting in Japan. It certainly made history very real to me that day.

Here are a few more War stories that Bob had mentioned to me over the years. The only time Bob ever went camping was with me in 1974. It wasn't really camping for Bob as he slept in the folded open back seat of a large Oldsmobile station wagon that his friend Jim Ellis, then an Oldsmobile dealer, let us borrow for the trip. I slept in a tent. Dad said he had had enough of tents in the War and would rather sleep in the car. Below is a photograph of some of the tent barracks he stayed in while in Europe and you can see why he slept in the car that trip.

On that same camping trip we went to Michigan's Upper Peninsula as neither of us had been there before. When driving along the very tall escarpment in the Keweenaw Peninsula at the furthest northern tip of Michigan with Lake Superior extending out forever toward the north, Bob said that it reminded him of the Chalk Cliffs of Dover. I hadn't heard that phrase before and he explained that it was a location in England along the English Channel that was always a welcome sight to him in the War as it meant leaving France or Germany and arriving back in the relative safety of England.

Another shot of tent barracks that Bob took during the War. Looks like some celebration was ready to happen what with the two bottles of wine in the foreground.

The last War story was told in 1972. I was 18 and my draft lottery date for the Viet Nam War had arrived. Bob and I never talked about it or the possible consequences for some reason. I don't recall really thinking much about the consequences myself. I guess that is why they draft 18-year olds. I ended up getting a very high number (327 out of 365) and they only drafted people up to number 200 or so that year, which, it turned out, was the last year that draftees actually went to Viet Nam to fight. I came home and told Dad I was off the hook. He said good, that he wouldn't have allowed me to go, that he would have sent me to Canada. I was shocked. In response to my look he said that, 'War is hell and I don't want my son to go through what I did."

"War is hell" Bob said. Bombed buildings he saw in Paris.

With camera in hand, Bob took some photographs of the devastation the War caused in Europe like the one above taken at an unknown location in Germany.

Bob was honorably discharged from the Army in late 1945 after serving in battles and campaigns in France, Holland, Belgium and Germany, not to mention bombed-out London. For reasons no longer known but probably understood, Bob did not make the Army his career like he had once thought of doing. Maybe it was the shell shock of the War. Maybe the need to settle down after five years in the military. Regardless, Bob had done his duty for his country.

It was the best of times, it was the worst of times.

He had paid back at least part of what America had given to him; the chance to be able to use his talents and personality to rise from poverty and obscurity to have fame and fortune, what truly exemplifies the American Dream. World War II didn't make Bob what he was or what he became. It just made him better, sharpened what he was and what he believed in. As to what it did to his interrupted golf career, well that is covered in the next chapter.

First, though, let's conclude this chapter on Bob's World War II experiences with some more photographs taken by him or of him as if they are not published here they will be forgotten and unseen by anyone other than me.

Allied soldiers on a military truck at an unknown location taken by Bob in World War II.

St. Augustine Church during the liberation of Paris.

Destroyed bridge, probably in Germany.

In front of a Parisian restaurant during World War II.

Bob with two other allied soldiers at an unknown location.

Bob outside of Army barracks with a friend.

Bob and friend outside of Officers' Mess in WWII.

Bob next to a staff car in Europe during World War II.

Bob posing next to a monument in Europe during WWII.

One last photograph from Bob's World War II packet of photographs, this one obviously taken in Brussels, Belgium at a checkpoint. Notice the sign is announcing a curfew and all cafes in town will close at 2200 hours (10 pm) and all the Army staff vehicles and Jeeps parked behind it.

# CHAPTER 7
# BACK INTO THE SWING OF THINGS: 1945 TO 1950

When Bob was honorably discharged from the Army in 1945 he didn't waste any time getting back into the swing of things as far as life and his golf game were concerned.

Still a bachelor, he moved in with brother John and his family on Collingham Street, living in the finished attic dormer upstairs. Bob did need some time to recover from the mental and physical side effects of being in the War and the one thing that helped him was getting back into a routine, his golf routine.

*Michigan Open —*
*Aug. 3 - 4 - 5 - 1945 -*

CAPT. ROBERT N. BABISH
U. S. Army
State Amateur Champion, 1935

"TOMMY" SHEEHAN
Amateur, Detroit
Runner-up Michigan Open, 1941
Former Inter-Collegiate Star at University of Notre Dame
Holds record as lowest qualifier in National Amateur Championships

Bob did play in a tournament in 1945. It was the Michigan Open in August. There is no record of how he did in it but that wasn't important; he was recovering from the War and playing golf again. The photograph on the prior page of Bob and Tommy Sheehan was an advertisement of them playing in that tournament. If you recall, Sheehan played for Notre Dame in college, graduating a year before Bob did.

Bob did go back to work for the tire company in Hartsville, Ohio late in 1945 when he returned from the War; they kept the job open for him while he was in the Army. While he was living in Ohio he was able to play some golf and get his game back into shape. This was seen by Bob qualifying for the U.S. Amateur Championship at Baltusrol Golf Club in Springfield, New Jersey in 1946, the first year it was held since 1942. There is no record of his performance at it though below is a photograph of Bob putting on the famous fourth hole of this course during this tournament while playing against Skee Reigel.

Bob also qualified for the U.S. Open Tournament in 1946, which was played in nearby Canterbury Country Club outside of Cleveland. The last time he had played in the U.S. Open was at the same course in 1940. Though it is lost to memory how Bob played in it that year, we do know that it was won by Lloyd Mangrum.

But, more importantly, Bob was back in the swing of things at the national golf level. The five-year war interruption didn't appear to have affected his game at all. The only difference now was that Bob was a "working stiff," as he used to call it, instead of a golf bum or collegiate.

Also in 1946, Bob made what was known as the Detroit District Golf Association's Honor Roll. This was the first time DDGA put this ranking of local amateur golfers out and it became an annual listing of the top players in Detroit for years. Back then it made headlines on the sports pages of the Detroit newspapers. It ranked Bob tenth overall with a one handicap. It stated that while Babbish played little tournament golf the previous summer, it was determined his recent records justified including him for that year.

Well, working for the tire company in Ohio didn't work out for Bob and he moved back to Detroit in late 1946. I never heard the reason why it didn't. I always wondered why Bob never moved down south. If he did he could have played golf all year round not just six or seven months then have to put away the clubs for winter. It must have been his love and loyalty for Detroit, the town that gave him the chance to go from obscurity to fame. It is hard to start new somewhere after all those years and succeed in another town and state and claw your way back to the top again.

Bob went to work as a car dealership salesman in

Detroit. His personality made him a great salesman and, as he found out, his golfing abilities didn't hurt either. As he had already moved out of John and Esther's house on Collingham to move to Ohio, he came back to Detroit and rented an apartment on Whitmore Street in the fancy Palmer Park Apartments, located at McNichols and Woodward Avenue and just a couple miles away from the U of D campus. He was still a very eligible bachelor and now he was even making money. I remember a story his roommate, Ben Smith, told at Bob's retirement party in 1984 about the apartment they shared there. He said that he had a very hard time collecting all the keys to the apartment that Bob had given out to the young women when Bob finally married in 1951. Bob also joined Red Run Golf Club in 1946.

With his move back to Detroit, Bob continued his golfing there in 1947. The DDGA Honor Roll for that year listed Bob as a scratch rating (0 handicap) and ranked as the Number 3 player in the rankings.

Bob again qualified for the U.S. Amateur in 1947. Qualifications for it were held at Oakland Hills and the tournament was at the Pebble Beach course near Del Monte, California. He qualified with seven other Detroit amateur golfers, including Chuck Kocsis and Tommy Sheehan, with a 148 in the qualification rounds. An article on the U.S. Amateur Qualifications that year bemoaned the fact that with eight Detroiters qualifying, only two of them were willing or able to make the trip to actually play in it. Remember, it was all the way out in California that year and most of them said that they didn't have the money to get out there. When asked if he was going, Bob was quoted in the paper as saying, "Nope."

Come 1948, Bob was ranked Number 1 in the DDGA honor roll. He also again qualified for and played in the

U.S. Open that was held at St. Louis Country Club in Ladue, Missouri that was won by Ben Hogan that year.

Bob played in the Detroit District Golf Association District Championship in 1949 and he was runner up to his roommate Ben Smith. Bob also won at least two local invitational tournaments that year. One of them that we have a record of was the Franklin Hills Country Club Invitational best-ball tournament. He teamed with member Bob Moers and won 3 and 1 in the finals. A newspaper article by Marshall Dann said that Bob "gave a convincing show in the title round. He birdied eight of the 17 holes in one of the finest clutch performances given locally this season. It erased some of the sting of the recent Detroit District finals when Babbish was humiliated by Ben Smith, 8 and 7, in an 18-hole match. Babbish birdied the third and sixth but didn't start his hot streak until the eighth. Then he birdied the eighth and ninth, where his team took a 1-up lead, and repeated on the 11th, 13th, 15th and 17th holes. The Babbish-Moers team finished six under par in the finals and 21 under par for the five rounds." His partner was just 22 years old and was playing in his first tournament. Knowing Bob, he was probably friends with the kid's father.

Bob also played in and won the Blythefield Country Club Invitational tournament in 1949 in Grand Rapids, MI.

Lastly for that year, Bob was runner-up in the DDGA Honor Roll in 1949.

So, Bob was back and it was as if he hadn't missed a golf swing. The one heartbreak in this post-war comeback was that he again was passed over for the Walker Cup team once it resumed playing the tournament in 1946. Same in 1949 when another Detroiter, Bob's friend Chuck Kocsis, made the team.

# CHAPTER 8
## BUSINESSMAN GOLF: 1950 TO 1960

In many ways, the decade of the 1950's was Bob's second career at golf. His post-war playing in the 1940's was a continuation of The Great Babbish and collegiate days in the 1930's, kind of continuing the "golf bum" life he had lived up to then. By 1950 Bob was settling down not only in golf but also in business and family life and was learning to successfully combine (or is the word "juggle"?) all three. Bob always said that the three most important things in his life were God, family and golf, and not necessarily in that order.

This, of course, meant less travel and playing more local tournaments. But now he could afford to play and, with his job as a salesman, he could play while he worked during the week by entertaining customers on the course. That was probably one reason he left the tire company in Ohio: he had a desk job there and Bob had to have a job that he could play golf on. Tournaments were usually on weekends and he didn't have to work then anyway. Bob remained an amateur golfer, as was his plan all along.

As we will see, the decade of the 1950's saw Bob stay on the national golf scene, largely by his continued ability to qualify for U.S. Open tournaments. He was still a big contender in the Detroit District sponsored tournaments and he continued to play and win a number of invitationals at local and even out-of-state golf clubs. He also married, had two children and worked at two different companies during this period. By the end of the decade, Bob was firmly established as one of the greatest golfers in Michigan as well as a successful businessman. Life was good.

A formal portrait of Bob the Businessman taken sometime
in the 1950's, probably in the middle of the decade when
he was working for the steel company. Notice the golf-
themed tie he was wearing and the quickly graying hair.

The decade started out with Bob being named the Number 5 player in the 1950 Detroit District Honor Roll based on his tournament play in 1949 and a 2 handicap. He was shown as still playing out of Red Run Golf Club in Royal Oak as he had been since he returned from Ohio in 1946.

Bob played in a tournament named the Motor City Open in 1950. It was held at his home club, Red Run, that year. This popular event, which wasn't played every year, was held for fifteen or so years at different Detroit area golf clubs and attracted many of the national professional golfers to it, thus its popularity among golf enthusiasts.

In a Detroit News article by Paul Chandler it said that, "Michigan had a pair of golfers in the Motor City Open who stayed local heroes to the finish: Jimmy Thompson and Bob Babbish. Babbish, who was one of the principal powers in Michigan amateur golf 10 years ago, led every amateur in the tournament by a margin of seven strokes and upward. In the whole field of golfers he finished eighth, just seven strokes behind champion Lloyd Mangrum, shooting a 281 on rounds of 70, 73, 69 and 69.

"His friends know that this year the 38-year-old car salesman dedicated himself to one last effort to see just what he could do with his golf game. Perhaps he was thinking it was possible to make the Walker Cup team. The Motor City Open provided the first real test, and he sailed through it magnificently. Babbish, who plays 95 per cent of his golf at Red Run and knows the course intimately, had 12 birdies and 5 bogies (all the rest were pars) on his 72 holes. He 'missed' only 11 greens. Babbish's triumph was an extremely popular victory." Bob was always proud of beating nationally known professional golfers Ben Hogan (by one shot), Cary Middlecoff, Gene Sarazen and Bob Toski at the 1950 Motor City Open.

**Red Run pro Frank Walsh (left) presents prize to Bob Babbish. Detroiter whose 281 was low for amateurs.**

Newspaper photo from the 1950 Motor City Open.

Bob played in the 1950 Michigan Amateur tournament held at Gull Lake Country Club outside of Kalamazoo, which was won by his friend Ben Smith. A newspaper article mentioned, again, that Bob was hoping his play in this tournament that year would allow him to be on the Walker Cup team. After qualifying easily, Bob was upset by Nap Chinick in the second round of match play.

Another big golf tournament win for Bob in 1950 was the Detroit District Golf Association Championship. A Detroit Free Press article dated August 7, 1950 by Marshall Dann said, "It was the major golf triumph of the season for Babbish, 35-year-old auto salesman who had his eye on a possible U.S. Walker Cup team berth.

"Babbish was three under par for 75 holes in progressing through the District field without strain. In turn, he beat Glenn Johnson, 3 and 2; Frank Connolly, 6 and 5; Lloyd Martz, another Red Runner in the semifinals, 6 and 5, and Dick Whiting. The only top-ranking player entered whom Babbish did not meet was Ben Smith, of Lochmoor. Smith, 1950 Michigan Amateur champ, won last year with an 8 and 7 rout over Babbish in the finals. This time Smith bowed to Whiting in the first round.

"The biggest surprise came in the morning match against Martz, who had been the hottest player in the tournament. Babbish had an eagle and two birdies on the first five holes in seizing a 3-up lead. He finished that match three under par, and then started against Whiting in the same fashion. In the first five holes, where he had another eagle and a birdie, Babbish again moved to a 3-up lead.

"Whiting took advantage of Babbish's only bogies, on the sixth and ninth, to win with pars and cut down the deficit to a single hole. But Babbish cashed in on Whiting's errors at the 12th and 13th to move out in front, lost the 14th to a birdie, and ended the match on the 16th. Although Babbish was even par in the finals, the caliber of play wasn't the best. Babbish's irons strayed at times, while Whiting got no help from his putting. Whiting failed to hole a single sizeable putt, and twice three-putted."

John Walter writing for The Detroit News said, "Pennsylvania-born Bob Babbish is Detroit District golf champion for the second time today. 'I won it for the *old men*' quipped the 35-year-old auto salesman after his 3-2 victory over red-headed Dick Whiting, his 27-year-old Red Run club mate at Lochmoor Golf Club Sunday. 'I guess I'm a 10-year-man' mused Babbish as he relaxed in the locker room. 'I won the District caddie championship in 1930, beat Chris Brinke for the District championship in 1940 and now here I'm District champion again in 1950.'

"He has scored other notable victories. He was state champion in 1935, Western Amateur titleholder in 1938. He was low amateur in the Motor City Open this year at Red Run. But he never has been able to get past the first round at the National Amateur. Three times he has been bumped in the first round.

"Babbish was behind only once in a match in the 75 holes he shot in two under par figures to win this year's tournament. In the final with Whiting he won three holes in a row, starting at No. 3, with a birdie-par-eagle, getting home in two on the 511-yard fifth for a five-foot putt for eagle. The only time Babbish was behind in the tournament after qualifying with a 75, was when Glenn Johnson, playing from Grosse Isle Golf Club, won the third hole with a birdie from him in the first round of play."

Bob also played in the U.S. Amateur Tournament held at the Minneapolis Golf Club for the fourth time that year, qualifying with a three under par 141 (69 and 72) having eight birdies, five bogeys and six traps at the Country Club of Detroit.

An article in the Detroit Free Press dated August 9, 1950 by Marshall Dann started off reading, "Bob Babbish, hard-campaigning Red Run amateur, annexed his second major golf triumph in three days. His latest honor was leading the National Amateur qualifying trials with a three-under-par 69-72 – 141 at Country Club of Detroit. Sunday he won the Detroit District crown at match play. Babbish, who was low amateur at the Motor City Open, topped the field of 29 starters by a single stroke." How Bob did at the actual National Amateur Tournament that year is not recalled.

One has to wonder the reason for this sudden burst of golfing activity and success for Bob in 1950. He was a "businessman golfer" at this point, holding a job down and playing golf when he could. As we will see next, it may have been because he knew that his life was going to take another turn and thought this was his last free year to really pursue golf. Plus that dream of playing on the Walker Cup team also seemed to have still been on his mind.

Starting off the year 1951 was Bob being ranked Number 1 on the DDGA annual Honor Roll list. In an article published in the Detroit Free Press dated May 6, 1951, writer Marshall Dann explained a bit about how the Honor Roll was compiled. "When compared with its handicap list, the DDGA's 1951 Honor Roll requires some explanation. Named as the Number 1 man on the Honor Roll was Bob Babbish, one of Red Run's many stars. Yet Babbish was topped by at least six other amateur golfers in the handicap computations. Here's the difference: The handicaps are figured on 1950 scoring while the Honor Roll is based on tournament performance as judged by a three-man committee. Babbish, with a one handicap while six others were rated a stroke better at scratch, was awarded the top spot on the Honor Roll for winning the District crown as well as leading in the National Amateur trials." The article noted that only Bob and Lloyd Martz have made the Honor Roll all the times it had been done.

Probably more important for Bob at this time was that he was dating and in love with a woman named Delphine

Kunkel from Hamtramck (that Polish city surrounded by the City of Detroit just a mile or so from where Bob grew up on Moenart Street) who was a recent Wayne State University graduate and was teaching in the Detroit Public Schools. Bob was introduced to Delphine by Woodrow W. Woody, a fellow golfer and owner of Woody Pontiac car dealership on Jos. Campau Street in Hamtramck who knew both families. Bob had been for years the most eligible bachelor in Detroit and maybe even Michigan. At thirty-five years old now, he realized it was the time to pursue one of his other dreams, to marry and have a family. He popped the question to Delphine one day and the rest is history.

Well, this was big news in Detroit and the sports and gossip pages of the local papers picked it up. Bob was no longer available and many women cried that day. Below is a clipping from a local Detroit newspaper in May 1951.

## Bob Babbish Will Marry on May 15

The ranks of Detroit's most-elibigle bachelors will lose its top golfer next week when Bob Babbish will be married.

Babbish, 35, will wed Miss Delphine M. Kunkel, 29, a teacher at the High School of Commerce. The couple obtained a marriage license Monday, and will be married May 15 at St. Florian's Church.

# Miss toMRS.

In a ceremony at St. Florian's church on Tuesday, May 15, Miss Delphine Kunkel, business department became the wife of Mr. Robert Babbish.

Mr. Babbish is the current Detroit District golf champion. He has held the Michigan Amateur and the Western Amateur crowns for the past 15 years. Mr. Babbish now holds the No. 1 position on the 1951 DDGA Honor Roll.

Mrs. Babbish plans to continue teaching at the High School of Commerce.

The above announcement after Bob's wedding was published in the Detroit Public School District teacher's newsletter and it is about Delphine as much as Bob. Bob and Delphine were married sixty-one years.

The first three years of their married life they lived in Bob's apartment in Whitmore Street in the Palmer Park Apartments. (Hopefully Bob got all those keys back by then.)

Bob and Delphine in their 1951 wedding photograph.

Also in 1951 Bob left Red Run Golf Club and joined Detroit Golf Club. As you recall, Bob at one time caddied at DGC and won the District Caddy Championship while there. This was another American Dream story of Bob's: The caddy succeeding in golf and business to become a member of the club he worked at as a kid. As a member of DGC, Bob was friends with everyone, members and workers alike. Not only was this because of his outgoing personality but also reflected the fact that he knew his roots as a poor, working class boy. He was always good to the caddies, giving them tips in the form of advice to become better caddies and in the form of a generous cash tip at the end of the loop. Bob was the member that all DGC caddies wanted to caddy for.

Bob also was close to all the staff working in the clubhouse, especially the cooking and wait staff. He never entered the DGC clubhouse by the main entrance or even the pro shop entrance. Instead, he came in through the employees' door that entered through the kitchen. When I used to accompany Bob there on weekends to caddy for him, we would come in the kitchen door. Sitting at the end of a counter was always a plate of pastries. I remember the first time we did this: Bob took one of the pastries, ate it in one bite, yelled to someone out of sight down the aisle, "Best ever, Cookie," told me to grab some of them, then we made our way up to the men's locker room. I asked him what was going on and he said that the pastry cook was diabetic and couldn't taste his own baked goods so he left a plate of them for Bob to taste when he arrived for his opinion of them. This happened every Saturday and Sunday morning for years.

Bob treated the men's locker room attendants, Steve and Larry, with respect and they took care of him probably better than any other member. There were always towels waiting for him by his locker and his golf shoes were shined, as were his street shoes when he was done playing. Same with mine when I was playing with him.

The waiters in the Men's Grill also loved him. Spiros and Chris, two long-time waiters there, tended to all his gastrointestinal needs as did Frank the bartender for his drinks. The cook handling the smorgasbord in the grill always knew what Bob would like from that day's offerings and would have a plate ready for him when he came up to eat. Though he less frequently visited the downstairs mixed grill or dining room, the staff there all knew and loved him too. After Bob consistently would make a request for a special sandwich, an onion and tomato sandwich, a favorite of Bob's from the Great Depression, the club kitchen staff eventually put it on the menu and called it *The Babbish* sandwich. It remained on the menu until the 1990's.

Bob was also friends with the workers who maintained the golf course itself, the "grounds crew." He knew each one by name and if he saw one he didn't know, a new hire, he made sure to get to know him. One long-time grounds worker was a mean-looking Russian immigrant named Paul. Every time he saw Bob on the course he would come over to him and they would have some heated discussion about politics of the Club, Detroit, United States or world. Bob seemed to enjoy these impromptu talks and called Paul the "Russian Radical."

When Bob would leave the Club for the day he would again go out a way that not many other members did. He went out through the Rack Room, the long narrow room where all the members' golf bags were stored. Steve Rybicki was the Rack Room Manager there forever and he and Bob used to caddy at DGC together so they went way back. Steve was a very good golfer and made a career at

DGC, retiring long long after normal retirement age. When I was done caddying and golfing and waiting for Bob to come down from the men's locker room to go home, I used to sit with Steve and hear all the old stories and help him wash arriving clubs and put them away in their racks.

Bob remained a member of DGC until he and Delphine retired and moved to Florida in 1984. He served on the Club's board of directors for many years. A trip there now reveals Bob's years as a member memorialized on the many plaques hung on the walls showing such information as club championships won and holes-in-one made.

Photo taken after a tournament in the 1950's at the table of honor for winners and runners-up. Bob is on far right.

In addition to marriage and honor rolls, Bob found the time to also qualify for the U.S. Open again in 1951, shooting a 72 and a 70 to do so. That year it was played at nearby Oakland Hills Country Club in Bloomfield Township, just northwest of Detroit. I recall Bob telling me that this was his best U.S. Open ever as, even though he didn't do as well in it as he had done in 1940 when he finished in 52$^{nd}$ place overall, he was the leading amateur after the first round that year. This was the tournament that prompted winner Ben Hogan to described Oakland Hills as "The Monster."

The year 1952 brought another chance at the DDGA District Championship played this year at Franklin Hills Country Club in Franklin, Michigan. Though he won medalist honors with shooting a 70 one round during the tournament, Bob lost to Dick Whiting, who got his revenge for his 1950 loss, in the finals. Bob had beaten Art Olff of Oakland Hills Golf Club in the semifinal round 6-5 at Red Run. He previously had defeated Glenn Johnson 2 up in the quarterfinals the day before at Franklin Hills Country Club.

### DISTRICT CHAMP AND TOP QUALIFIERS

Detroit Times Photo

Ben Smith (left), who starts defense of district title today with top scorers | in qualifier: Tony Novitsky, 71, one under par, and the medalist, Bob Babbish, 70.

An article by M. F. Drukenbrod written during the qualification rounds held at Franklin Hills Country Club for the contest said, "Babbish, who collected six birdies against four bogeys, was favored by a good break on the par 5 fourth. He sailed his third over the green and headed for out of bounds. But the ball hit a tree and bounded back in. This enabled him to salvage a most welcome bogey 6. But it was his putting which really put Babbish over. Babbish narrowly missed driving into the lake on 18 and had to play his second over a tree. He was short of the green but a good chip gave him the par 4 he needed to edge out Tony Novitsky."

In another article about this tournament it is said that Bob gave the trophy he was awarded for medalist honors, an elaborate ash tray sporting the figure of a golfer, to his friend Byron (Bud) C. Gould also of the Detroit Golf Club. "Babbish was complaining about his putting to Gould before he teed off. Checking up, Gould found Babbish had been missing all his putts to the right. He quickly showed Babbish that was because he had his left hip turned slightly to the right, partially blocking his putting stroke. Making sure his hips were parallel with the putting line, Babbish immediately improved. He sank 20-foot putts for three consecutive birdies in the qualifying round, starting at the fifth hole, birdied No. 10 and 11 with putts of 10 and 15 feet, respectively."

This was the first mention of Bud Gould I came across. Bud was the president of Murray Corporation, a large company located in Detroit that, at that time, made large home appliances like washing machines. Bud and Bob knew each other from the Detroit Golf Club and is another example of how golf transcended all social/economic lines in America. Bud was a wealthy businessman and Bob a golfer and the love of golf was the only thing they had in common. They became great friends and a great golfing team. We will be hearing a lot about Bud throughout this chapter.

I do not have any clippings about the DDGA Honor Roll for 1952 so do not know how Bob was ranked that year. However, Bob did win a tournament in Pennsylvania in 1952. It was the Bill Waite Memorial best ball golf championship sponsored by Fred Waring and was played at the Shawnee Inn and Golf Resort.

Bob was very good friends with Fred Waring, a popular musician and bandleader of the *Pennsylvanians* who had a show on television and radio at this time known as *The Fred Waring Show*. Bob was often invited by Fred to attend the television show broadcasts and concerts in New York City and invited Bob to play in his annual golf tournament at the Shawnee Inn and Golf Resort.

Bob played in this Fred Waring-sponsored tournament many times in the 1950's. I recall him telling me that you had to take a train to get there from Detroit as there was no other way to do so other than drive. Fred treated Bob like a dignitary when he was in town and often invited him and his wife down to Shawnee on the Delaware on weekends just to play golf. Other times Bob and Delphine would fly or take the train into New York to attend a concert or taping of *The Fred Waring Show* then head back to Shawnee on the Delaware for some golf.

This Fred Waring connection was another, new level of social status that golf brought to Bob. The relationship wasn't one created by business but by golf. Fred had heard about Bob's golfing skills and was charmed by Bob when they first met. Golf was the means of propelling Bob from his simple, humble origins to mingling with the rich and famous, which we will see more of a bit later in this chapter with other famous celebrities. Of course, Bob's outgoing personality helped too.

Howard Everitt, from Atlantic City, and Bob, the winners
of the 1952 Bill Waite Memorial tournament hosted by
Fred Waring at Shawnee Inn and Country Club.

Bob again qualified for the National Amateur Tournament in 1953, which was to be held at Brookline, Massachusetts. He was the medalist at qualification with the low score of 146 with a 71 and a 75 around the 6,910-yard par 72 Country Club of Detroit course in Grosse Pointe. Bob was quoted in an article as saying, "With the strong wind this course played mighty long for an old man like me." Asked whether he will make the trip to the tournament he said, "It depends upon business and family matters whether I'll go." He did play in it and went to the third round in the actual tournament that year, his best finish yet. He also was low amateur in that year's Michigan Open Tournament.

The big golf news for 1953 was Bob winning the Detroit District Golf Association's District Championship for the third time. The 36-hole finals were held at Meadowbrook Country Club and Bob was playing Roy Iceberg, a public links player versus Bob belonging to a golf club. There were a lot of articles in the newspapers covering each day of that tournament.

An article after the semifinals in the Detroit Free Press by Marshall Dann mentioned that Iceberg, then 31, was a former Lochmoor Country Club caddy and that he qualified to play in this tournament usually reserved for members of golf clubs by winning the 1952 Michigan Public Links Championship. It also said that Bob staged a dramatic come-from-behind rally and then went into an extra holes playoff to stop Tom Draper, one up, in 20 holes in the semifinals.

I have four articles about Bob winning it in the finals (which is odd as there were only three newspapers in town then and Marshall Dann wrote two of the articles), pretty good coverage of a local tournament. It took 39 holes to win, including the three playoff holes to break the tie after

the normal 36 holes, and Bob could have won on the last
hole in regulation but he missed a 2-foot putt there
allowing the tie and the playoff holes. He was leading 1-up
after 35 holes and only need to match Iceberg's score on
the last scheduled hole. An article by Harry Stapler
described what happened. "The 38-year-old steel executive
putted quickly. The ball shied from the lip on the right side
and passed the cup. A woman shouted, 'He got it, he got
it.' She was shouting about Iceberg winning the hole, not
Babbish's putt. It was almost inconceivable that Babbish,
champion in 1940 and 1950 and once a state amateur
champion, should have blown such a brief putt. Babbish
looked at the woman sharply and walked to the 37th tee for
the playoff.

"This was the test for Babbish. The pressure had
shifted to him from Iceberg, who with only five holes to go
had been three down. Babbish, the steadier golfer by a
slender amount all day, didn't melt. Iceberg did, on the 39th
of the sudden death, overtime duel by landing in a trap on
his second shot and missing his 30-foot putt whereas Bob
landed his ball on the green in two strokes, his first putt
landing two feet from the cup and not making the same
mistake on 36 by making this putt for the win. About the
missed putt on 36, Bob said, 'I guess I hurried. I didn't
want to give myself time to think – it only takes a second to
miss.' "

There was a side article by M. F. Drukenbrod about
Bob changing putters midstream during the tournament.
"If you want to win a golf championship, here's a
suggestion: come armed with two putters. Bob Babbish
did that yesterday an Meadowbrook Country Club and it
helped the Detroit star defeat Roy Iceberg. It was
Babbish's third triumph in five appearances in this
tournament' final (1940, 1950, 1951, 1952 and 1953) and it

**BOB BABBISH**
In finals fifth time, he wins third title

*BABBISH BEATS ICEBERG*

# Muffs 2-Footer, but He's Champ

followed one of the most exciting and best played finals in the event's long history. Getting no place with his blade putter early on in the morning round, Babbish switched to a mallet-headed one at the eighth. To make room for the extra putter he carried only two woods, a driver and a 4-wood. The second putter worked so well that he needed only 11 putts, including a 30-footer to birdie 10 and an 18-footer he rolled in on top of Iceberg's 25-footer to halve the fifteenth. Oddly, had he lost on extra holes, Babbish could have blamed his defeat on putter No. 2 as he muffed a 30-incher with it at the 36th hole and Iceberg won it to square the match" and force sudden death. Two of the articles mentioned something about Bob's personal life. Both articles said that he was a "sales manager for a steel firm." This was a recent job change for Bob, one that would turn out to be very good for him business-wise.

Bob also played in the Motor City Open in 1953. All we have of that event is the photograph appearing on the next page.

The other tournaments Bob played in that year were all golf club invitationals where he was paired with a club member that invited him to play. You can imagine that Bob was in big demand for these invitationals, what with his golf skills and record. It was often the only time a club member could win a tournament and the concurrent bragging rights and Bob played in a lot of these over the years.

Of the invitationals we know Bob played in that year, one was the second annual Orchard Lake Country Club Best-Ball Invitational. This was a return twenty-three years later of the one-time Orchard Lake caddy, where Bob's team won the caddy districts in 1930. At this tournament Bob and member Chase Morsey won with a 64. Bob took low gross honors for guests with a 67 that day.

# Red Run Pro Checks Scores

Free Press Photo

Pro Frank Walsh (left) checks the scores of Jim McKnight and Bob Bobbish (right), Red Run Golf Club members, after they had completed their 18 holes in the qualifying round of the invitational tournament at Red Run. The championship play will start Friday with the finals carded for Sunday.

A photograph taken of Bob at the 1953 Motor City Open Tournament held at Red Run Golf Club.

We know that Bob qualified for the 1953 U.S. Open golf tournament, his seventh time, and that he played in it but we do not know how he did in it. Ben Hogan won it again that year and it was held at Oakmont Golf Club in Oakmont, Pennsylvania just outside of Pittsburgh.

Bob also played in and won the Red Run Golf Club Invitational in 1953, playing with his friend Bud Gould. A short article about it said that, "Bob Babbish came up with one of the surest, if not THE surest, ways to end an extra-hole match in the first round of the Red Run Invitational Tournament. He fired an eagle-3 on the nineteenth to win for himself and Bud Gould over Harold Stewart and Paul Jackson."

Bob and Bud Gould also competed in the Blythefield Country Club Invitational in Grand Rapids, Michigan in June 1953 and won it for the second time. The Grand Rapids papers covered the tournament heavily and I have two articles from The Grand Rapids Press and The Grand Rapids Herald Tribune both dated Friday, June 12 that covered the second round held that day.

The article in The Grand Rapids Press by Clank Stoppels started off saying, "Scorching scores continued to be the feature of the eleventh annual Blythefield Invitational Golf Tournament as the event moved into its second round. Bob Babbish and Bud Gould, both of Detroit, who set a blistering seven-under-par 65 pace Thursday, picked up right where they left off Friday morning. They carved out four birdies on the 3,290-yard first nine holes. They already had a three-shot lead over the field as they teed off Friday morning and there are those who believe there is no catching them now." The article mentioned Bob hitting "a tremendous" 330-yard drive on the 400-yard ninth hole.

CHAMPIONS AT WORK—The two teams pictured above have won past Blythefield Invitational titles. At left, Bob Babbish slams a drive off the fourteenth tee while his partner, Bud Gould, also of Detroit, watches. They set qualifying pace Thursday with a seven-

So, as you can see, "businessman golf" was going rather well for Bob so far this decade. Being an executive for a steel company now gave Bob more opportunities to play golf "on the job" with customers than selling cars did prior to this. That was probably the reason why his friend, Sol Eisenberg, hired Bob to work for his steel company in Detroit.

Probably the biggest event for Bob in 1953, if I do say so myself, was the birth of his first child. That was me. Married for two and a half years by then, now he was a father, a role he took very seriously but which he tried not to let interfere with golf. I mentioned Bud Gould a few times. I was named Byron after him (his real first name). I also had the same middle initial "C" as Bud did but it was after another friend of Bob's: Charlie Escoe. Charlie worked for the Detroit Tigers baseball team in ticket sales and always had extra game tickets to give to Bob. A story from more recent times is when I was a father I went down to the old Tiger Stadium box office one day to purchase tickets to take my family to an upcoming game. While at the ticket window I asked if Charlie Escoe still worked there. The man inside, who was about my age, said no, that his Dad had retired. I said, "Dad?" and he said he was Matt Escoe, Charlie's son and who was I? I introduced myself and he said, "How is Uncle Bob?"

Bud Gould and his wife Billie never had any children of their own. Bud was very wealthy from his job as president of Murray Corporation. I remember that Billie, who was also good friends with Delphine, always drove a black Cadillac and whenever I see one from that timeframe of 1949 to mid-1950's, that classic style with the small fins on it, I think of her car which made an impression on me very early in life. Bob once mentioned to me that, even though Bud and he were good friends, one of the reasons he named me after him was that he had hoped that Bud, not having his own children, would "take care of me" as his namesake. I even called him "Uncle Bud." Well, I can tell you that never happened but all for the best as I took care of myself. Bob did well in business but, coming from a poor background, he was always looking for ways to have his son's life better and this was one of them. Glad it didn't work out as planned.

Come 1954 Bob was pretty much on top of the world, what with being a father, having a new job at the steel company and coming off a very successful golf season the prior year. First of all that year was the results of the DDGA Honor Roll. Bob came in as the Number 2 golfer by winning the District Championship and the Red Run Invitational the prior year as well as being low amateur in the Michigan Open and qualifying for the U.S. Open. This marked the eighth straight year that Bob had earned a spot on the Honor Roll and thus was the only player to be represented on every Honor Roll since the selections were started. Number 1 in 1954 was Ray Palmer of Grosse Isle.

In February 1954, Bob played in his first Bing Crosby National Pro-Am Golf Championship, also known as the *Crosby Clambake*. It was played at the four courses at Pebble Beach, California. I do not know how he was invited to play in this event that year but it was probably the Bud Gould connection. It looks like he was there with at least one other Detroit Golf Club member, Dr. Donald Jaffar. On the next page is a photograph taken of Bob and Dr. Jaffar at that event. This is all that is remembered of Bob playing there that year. It was the first of three times he did so. More on those other times later.

Bob, on far right, and friend and fellow DGC member Dr. Jaffar, second from left, at the 1954 Bing Crosby National Pro-Am at Pebble Beach with their unrecalled pros.

Bob competed in and won the Pine Lake Country Club Invitational tournament that year, beating Ralph Ellstrom. He also won for the first time the Detroit Golf Club Club Championship, which was for members only, the first of three such victories at his home course.

Additionally, Bob, playing with Bud Gould again, won the 1954 Red Run Golf Club Invitational for the second time in two years. John Walter of The Detroit News reported: "Fifteen stroke under par for 83 holes. That was the sensational golf collaborated on by Bob Babbish and Bud Gould, of the Detroit Golf Club, to capture Red Run's 13th annual best ball invitation tournament. Gould, a five-handicap player, gave Babbish some notable help as they triumphed over the Linklater brothers, George and Harry, in the final, 3-2. They were all even after 11 holes. Then the Detroit Golf Club pair took three holes running."

As defending champion, the big 1954 tournament for Bob was again the Detroit District Golf Association District Championship, this time at Pine Lake Country Club in West Bloomfield Township. As usual, this tournament was widely covered by the Detroit newspaper with articles written for the quarterfinal, semifinal and final rounds. As you will see, Bob won it for the fourth time.

Marshall Dann wrote about the quarterfinal round; "Defending Champion Bob Babbish shot his way into the semifinals Saturday in the Detroit District Golf Championship to reach that round for the fourth time in five years. He was joined by Glenn Johnson, the current Michigan Amateur champ, and two veterans, Frank Connolly and Ralph Ellstrom. Bob shot subpar golf for the third straight round to defeat Art Olfs, 2 and 1. The 39-year-old veteran from Detroit Golf Club birdied the first three holes and was four up after five before Olfs got started."

Bob then played Glenn Johnson in the semifinals of the 1954 DDGA District Championship. He beat Glenn 5 and 3. Bob opened with a birdie-par-birdie on the first three holes for another quick lead like he had in the quarterfinals. In four matches over the years, Glenn had never beaten Bob. This would change starting next year.

Bob Babbish: He Has a Title to Defend

Photograph from Detroit newspaper showing Bob in the
1954 Detroit District Golf Association District
Championship.

Bob played against 40 year-old Ralph Ellstrom of Dearborn Country Club in the rainy 36-hole finals at the DDGA District Championship at Pine Lake Country Club. An article written for a local newspaper by Harry Stapler began, "Bob Babbish, a one-time caddy and now a steel salesman, has towered over his amateur golf record near the peak held by Chuck Kocsis in Chuck's more active tournament summers." The article continued, "Babbish, of Detroit Golf Club, became the 1954 Detroit District champion yesterday, not unexpectedly so. He had been champion three other years. In his infrequent appearances in Michigan's major amateur tournaments, this is Babbish's record: District: 7 starts, 4 wins, 2 runner-ups. State Amateur: 6 starts, 1 win, 3 runner-ups. He has reached the finals ten times in these 13 match play efforts, a phenomenal percentage. In yesterday's sprinkling rain at Pine Lake, Babbish defeated Ellstrom 4 and 3. Babbish had led 1-up after the morning's 18 holes and won three quick holes early in the afternoon round. Ellstrom's spurts thereafter were never enough to catch Babbish."

In another article by M. F. Drukenbrod it said that the one-time caddy, "Carried off a big one. The triumph looms especially large because it matched the record of Chris Brinke, the tournament's only other four-time winner. Only his 1938 Western Amateur championship could possibly stand out above yesterday. Bob is the only Detroiter to ever win the Western. Babbish, 39 and now a weekend golfer, promised to come back again next year and seek a record fifth district title."

The Detroit Golf Club's newsletter also wrote up Bob's victory noting that, "Now Babbish's name is recorded on the handsome K. T. Keller Trophy four times. Chris Brinke, also a four-time winner, wrote Babbish a letter of congratulations on his victory, adding that he hoped

Babbish continued his fine play in the U.S. Amateur qualifying at the Country Club of Detroit. 'It's nice to know that the old men are playing pretty good' was Babbish's response to Brinke. 'And if I hit 'em through the trees at the Country Club as good as I did at Pine Lake, I might go some place.' "

Lastly, Bob did qualify to play in the U.S. Amateur at the Country Club of Detroit later that summer of 1954 and he made it to the third round in the actual tournament. The winner that year? A young upstart from Pennsylvania named Arnold Palmer.

Bob the businessman golfer (far right) with friends at some event in the 1950's, including college buddy Jim "Zip" Ellis (next to Bob). I like those double-breasted suits they are all wearing and the kerchiefs in the pockets.

"On the basis of their 1954 feats, Glenn Johnson and Bob Babbish, winners of two outstanding amateur tournaments in the state last season, become logical leadoff men on the annual Honor Roll of the Detroit District Golf Association. Often this annual procedure touches off arguments and controversy, but not this year." So started the newspaper article written by Marshall Dann about the 1955 DDGA Honor Roll. Glenn was ranked Number 1 and Bob Number 2 that year.

Bob played in the Michigan Open Championship in 1955, loosing for the first time ever to Glenn Johnson in the semifinals. This was the first of three tournaments that Glenn beat Bob in 1955.

Bob was then a surprise, last minute entry in the 1955 Michigan Amateur being played at Jackson Country Club. In a Detroit Free Press article dated Monday, July 11, 1955, it said, "Bob Babbish is going to bid once more for a title he held exactly 20 years ago. The current Detroit District champion, Babbish filed a surprise entry Sunday for the 1955 Michigan Amateur championship, which starts in Jackson on Wednesday."

"The graying, 40-year-old Detroit Golf Club star quickly was established as the favorite. Babbish won the 1935 Amateur crown, defeating Ed Nowak in the finals. He was runner-up three other times, losing in the finals to Chuck Kocsis in 1934 and 1937 and to Dave Ward in 1936. The powerful hitter with an unorthodox swing, Babbish made his last appearance in this event in 1950 at Gull Lake near Kalamazoo. That was a memorable performance. After qualifying easily, he was upset by Nap Chinick in the second round of match play."

"Babbish will be among the 300 challengers to Glenn Johnson who won here a year ago. Entries were accepted until 5 pm on Monday."

—Citizen Patriot Photograph.

BEFORE THE BATTLE BEGINS—Harold Brink of Grand Rapids, left, and Bob Babbish of Detroit, two of the state's finest golfers, are friends off the golf course. But they'll be all business Saturday when they clash in the feature match of the third round of the Michigan amateur tournament at the Country club. They last met in the tournament in 1935, Babbish winning on his march to the title.

An article about the beginning of the third round in the tournament appearing in the Jackson Citizen Patriot by Al Cotton, Sports Editor, had the above photograph with it and it was titled "Veterans End All Youthful Threats in Tournament." It stated, "The veterans are not yet ready to let the youngsters take over the Michigan Amateur Golf Tournament. As the tournament entered its third round Saturday at the Jackson Country Club, the field reduced from 315 to 16, it was a solidly veteran array of shot makers who began operations against each other."

Another article by Al Cotton the next day had the following headline blazed across the front page of the sports section: "Johnson Faces Babbish in State Golf Semi-Final." The article said, "Glenn Johnson, the champion from Grosse Isle, and Bob Babbish, champion in 1935, are each in the semi-finals to be held at Jackson Country Club today. Johnson, in the semi-finals for the fourth straight year, winner of his last 10 matches in the state and 20 of 24 in the four-year period, is determined to beat the portly, graying 40-year-old Babbish should they make the finals. The tournament "experts" favor Babbish, pointing out that he has beaten Johnson in Detroit District tournaments in the last two years."

The article went on with a definite bias towards Glenn Johnson, the "muscular" one-time Michigan State University quarterback, saying about Bob: "Babbish, whose unorthodox golfing form is nothing to breed confidence, although his experience, short game and putting are, passed his big test to date in the tournament when he edged Harold Brink, Grand Rapids veteran, 1 up in his morning round. Then he came on to shoot two under par golf and dispose of Cliff Taylor, of Muskegon, 4 and 3 in the afternoon. Babbish plays a big game in his powerful arms and when he really uncorks a drive it isn't uncommon for him to jump with both feet. But he has won many championships."

Funny that he mentioned the "Babbish Jump." Bob certainly did jump on his drives from the tee. It was his way of putting his whole body into the big shot. He did not jump on any other shots. When he was done with the swing he was literally facing the fairway with his body. As he learned golf on his own as a caddy he never had anyone teach him the proper swing and this worked for distance.

ONLY ONE CAN WIN IT TODAY—The four remaining players in the Michigan amateur golf championship at the Country club all have designs on the famous old stag horn trophy, but only one can win it this afternoon. Left to right, Ed Ervasti of Royal Oak who won it in 1947 but has lost in the finals the past two years; John Kurach, of Detroit, in his first state tournament; Glenn Johnson of Grosse Ile, who held the trophy the past year and wants to keep it in his possession, and Bob Babbish, of Detroit, who put his name on the trophy when he won the title in 1935. Babbish plays Johnson Sunday morning and Kurach opposes Ervasti. The two winners clash in the final Sunday afternoon at 2.

—Citizen Patriot Photograph

Glenn and Bob won their quarterfinal matches, Bob beating long-time foe Dick Whiting, the 1952 champion from Red Run, 1 up and Glenn beating Wally Smith 3 and 2 on Saturday.

So Glenn and Bob met in the semifinals that year. In an article in the August 7, 1955 Detroit Sunday Times, writer Lewis H. Walter wrote, "Weighing up Sunday's semifinal, Johnson said, 'Well, Babbish hasn't beaten me yet this year.' They have met once this season. A month ago Johnson conquered Babbish, 1 up, in the semifinals of the state championship. It is the only victory he boasts over the Detroit Golf Club player."

Johnson beat Bob in the semifinals that year, 1-up.

The next big tournament was the Detroit District Championship that was held in August 1955 at Orchard Lake Country Club. This tournament garnered a lot of attention not only because if Bob won he would be the only player to have won it five times, having won it the last two years in a row, but because of what was being called the Glenn Johnson/Bob Babbish "feud." Glenn was finally getting the upper hand on Bob this year, defeating him twice that summer.

There were a few articles written before the tournament even begun. Harry Stapler wrote one of them for a Detroit newspaper entitled, "After 40 Years, Swing is Sure." "When they say life begins at 40, they must be talking about a man's golf swing. Of the golfers who began contending today for the Detroit District Championship, nearly one-third have passed their 40th birthday. Of them, Bob Babbish is plainly the best known in Detroit amateur golf. As defending champion, he led the field of 32 this morning onto Orchard Lake Country Club. He learned to play there as a caddy in 1926.

" 'Hitchhiking out here from the east side of Detroit in those days was tough – no traffic,' he recalled. 'But we used to do it even if it took all day.' It is curious that Babbish has monopolized the district championship two straight years. For some time he has been what they call a 'business golfer.'

" 'There's not enough time for tournaments,' explained the 40-year-old steel salesman. 'I play a lot, but mostly with business acquaintances. I had only 20 minutes on the practice tee yesterday. That was at best just a warm-up. Some fellows like Glenn Johnson spend two hours there.' "

FRIDAY, AUGUST 5, 1955

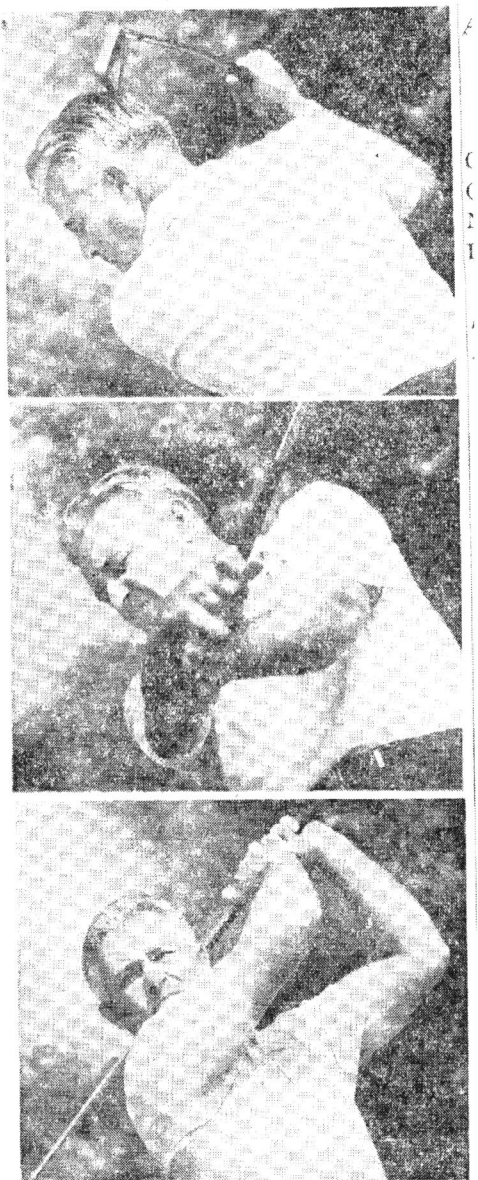

## SPECIALIST IN IRONS

Steel salesman Bob Babbish, regarded as one of the state's finest iron players, demonstrates for The News' 70 mm Hulcher sequence camera how he handles a No. 4 iron—at the peak of his backswing, powering through the ball and following through. Babbish is defending champion in the Detroit District championship. *(Story on Page 42.)*

The same article went on to say, "Babbish is extremely efficient with his irons and putter. Some have observed his way of lining up an iron shot. 'Whenever I feel I'm playing badly I invariably find I'm hitting to the right,' explained Bob. 'Like a lot of others, I'm right-eyed.' So he often steps well behind the ball and lays his iron on the ground, sighting the handle through the ball to his target. He stands with his toes against the club handle to establish an accurate stance. [Editor's Note: Bob was really "left-eyed."]

"Babbish now limits his major golf work to the district tournament, which he has won four times, and an occasional state tournament. When active before World War II, he won the district, state and Western Amateur championships."

Bob won his opening match, defeating Dr. G. R. Schwarz of Lakelands 5 and 4. So did Glenn Johnson, beating Ralph Ellstrom of Dearborn 3 and 2. In an article written by Lewis H. Walter before the quarterfinals, he said, "The possibility that Detroit District Golf Champion Bob Babbish and State Champion Glenn Johnson will carry their golfing feud to another showdown is nearer reality. Both are favored today as they enter their quarterfinal matches in the District championship at Orchard Lake Country Club. Babbish, 40, and Johnson, 32, are in opposite brackets, trying to shoot their way into the championship final of 36 holes to be played tomorrow.

"Babbish and Johnson have met four straight times in the District tournament. Each time Babbish, the stocky manufacturer's agent who is four-time champion, has conquered the 32-year-old insurance agency partner from Grosse Isle. Johnson, however, believes he reversed the trend when he finally downed Babbish 2 up in the State Amateur championship at Jackson last month.

Shawnee 1951

Here is a great photograph of the two "feuding" amateurs, Glenn Johnson and Bob, taken a bit earlier at a Fred Waring tournament at Shawnee Golf Resort in Pennsylvania. Bob and Glenn were great friends.

"Babbish's form is hard to judge because the Detroit Golf Club veteran plays a leisurely game, often just enough to win. That was the way he played as he went three over par in winning 5 and 4 in the first round yesterday. Then Babbish had to put on the pressure to beat the slender, serious Dave MacHarg of Dearborn, 1 up in 19 holes. He did it with a 15-foot birdie putt on the extra hole after MacHarg had squared their match by putting his approach shot eight inches from the pin for a birdie at No 18. Babbish was two under par for the 19 holes."

As you probably guessed, Bob faced Glenn in the finals. The feud that the newspapers were playing up fell right into their laps and they made the most of it.

In one article it said, "Those who play percentages must stick with Bob Babbish, perennial finalist, when he faces Glenn Johnson Sunday in the 36-hole match for the Detroit District Golf Association championship. Those who side with youth must pick Johnson. 'Babbish is the only fellow who's ever beaten me in the District Tournament and he's done it four years in a row,' explained Johnson after he and Babbish won semi-final matches at Orchard Lake Country Club Saturday afternoon. Johnson's supporters, however, recall that three weeks ago at Jackson their man beat Babbish in the semi-finals of the State Amateur championship. That's the only time in match play Johnson has ever bettered Babbish. Certainly these are Michigan's best two amateurs."

In another pre-finals article written by Marshall Dann in the August 7, 1955 Detroit Free Press, it said, "It is a meeting calculated to pack more interest than any local amateur match in many years. Two strong winning streaks will be going. Then there is their personal feud. Babbish met and defeated Johnson in each of the last four District tournaments. Johnson finally broke the spell with a 1-up conquest in the State championship just three weeks ago.

Sunday, August 8, 1955 was the big day of the District finals. As written again by Marshall Dann for the Detroit Free Press, "Their match was a see-saw affair, neither getting more than a 1-up lead for 33 holes. Johnson had the lead five times but could not hold it. Babbish, who was ahead twice, squared the match on the 32nd hole.

"Then it swung in Johnson's favor with dramatic suddenness. After the two had carefully played a total of 267 shots, two successive shots brought Johnson to victory. On the 446-yard 15th, Babbish missed an eight-foot putt needed to halve the hole. Johnson went 1-up again. Next shot played was Johnson's six-iron off the tee at the 155-yard 16th. It rolled just 12 inches past the cup. Babbish needed a 45-footer to match that. He missed and Johnson was 2-up.

"It ended on the next green when Johnson tapped in a five-footer for the par that cinched victory. Defeat snapped Babbish's string of 14 consecutive match-play victories in the District meet, a string that carried him to the 1953 and 1954 titles and to the finals this time."

LINKS SWEEP is chalked up by Glenn Johnson (right) as he defeats Bob Babbish, 2 and 1, for the Detroit District golf championship. Johnson earlier won the State Amateur. (See Story on Page 28.)

Also in 1955, Bob played in and reached the semifinals of the Michigan Open Championship. He again was beaten by Glenn Johnson. He also played in the inaugural Dearborn Country Club Invitational Best Ball golf tournament, which he won with member George Hain. One article about this tournament called Bob the "unofficial Detroit area champion amateur."

So what do we get out of Bob's 1955 golf year? That 1954 was probably his peak year of golf, certainly in the post-war era. He turned 40 in 1955 and was being beaten by a man eight years younger. The baton was handed over that year, which is remarkable in that it took so long to do so. Obviously, Bob wasn't happy about it. After such a great 1954 he had planned on continuing his golfing successes at least one more year. But when you are on top you are a target and the younger sharpshooting gunslingers finally hit their mark that year. Plus the younger players were more athletic than Bob ever was. The only time I ever heard of Bob exercising was his handball sport in college. He figured that walking 18 to 36 holes a day golfing was plenty enough exercise. And, the next generation coming up also seemed to play the sport not so much for the fun of it, as Bob's generation did, but for the fame, glory and prestige.

This did not mean the end of competitive golf for Bob. As we will see, he remained competitive throughout the decade at the state and national level. After that, though, his tournament focus switched to the local club level tournaments, which he was working into now. As Bob said, being a businessman golfer was nice but it did mean less time to practice. And there also was that family he had now.

Speaking of his family, Bob and Delphine moved into his apartment in Whitemore Street when they married in

1951 but it turns out that no children were allowed in his building and I was born in December 1953. Well, they somehow kept me hidden from the authorities for a while but got asked to move out in 1954. Bob bought a house on Muirland Street about two miles away from his Palmer Park apartment and one street east of the University of Detroit.

Here is Bob's first house on Muirland Street in a photograph taken in December 1959, their last year there. That is the six-year-old author on the porch with him.

Though young at that time, I have fond memories of this house and growing up in it. As you know, Bob's brother John was a fireman, something I was very impressed with when young (I still have his old fireman's metal helmet from way back then). For a while he was assigned to the firehouse that covered my neighborhood.

One day I heard a siren outside the house. I ran to the door and parked out front was a hook and ladder fire truck with its lights flashing and a fireman walking towards the door in full gear waving at me. Not noticing it was Uncle John, I screamed to Mom that the house was on fire and we needed to get out, that a fireman was coming to rescue us! When I finally realized the fireman was Uncle John and found out that he was on his way back from a fire and thought he would stop by to show me the fire truck, I was too embarrassed to really enjoy that unique opportunity.

Another time while living in Muirland we were having a family party in the back yard one evening and a thunderstorm was approaching. The thunder and lightning was scaring me and Bob took me in his arms, pointed to the dark sky and said that it was only God up there bowling, the noise and lightning was when he got a strike. I still think of that to this day whenever we have a bad storm.

After moving into Muirland, Bob purchased Delphine her first car. It was a 1955 Chevrolet Bel Aire. We had a sloping driveway but no garage. One day my neighbor Brian McHale and I were sitting on the fender of the Chevy while it was parked at the top of the driveway. Suddenly it started rolling down the driveway! Delphine must not have put the parking brake on (it had a manual transmission) and Brian and I watched in horror as it gained speed rolling down approaching Muirland Street. I vividly remember thinking that the car would blow up when it reached the street and went running into the house yelling to Mom that her car is going to blow up, do something Mom! Mom ran out and we all saw the car cross Muirland, roll partially up the neighbor's driveway across the street then roll back down and eventually settle in the middle of the street. No harm done but I guess I had been watching too much TV by then and was expecting (or hoping for) the worse.

One last Muirland story. One day I was out in the backyard and in the distance I heard a loud thumping sound that grew louder. Soon the sky was filled with helicopters, all really low and flying slowly. I could feel the wind from their blades. I went running in yelling to Bob, who wasn't working or golfing for some reason that day, that we were being attacked! The Communists have arrived! Again, TV was becoming more accessible back then and I was a big user of it, fueling my imagination. Bob came out, looked up and said it was OK, that they were landing on the U of D property a block away for some National Guard exercise. Wish he would have told me that earlier. After the last helicopter had landed Bob and I walked the block there to see all the activity. That was very exciting to a kid like me.

The year 1956 started the shift to playing more golf club invitational tournaments for Bob. This included some outside of Michigan, something that he had done a lot of years ago but not so much in this decade. Bob did not play in the Detroit District or the Michigan Amateur tournaments after 1955 as far as I can tell.

Bob did compete in the second annual Detroit Medal Play Tournament in 1956 and won it. It was the Bob's first year playing in this tournament that was held at Red Run Golf Club, his old home course. In a short article entitled, "Quick Birdie Wins Playoff for Babbish," it said, "Bob Babbish won a three-way playoff to gain his first Detroit Medal Play championship yesterday after deadlocking at the end of 72 holes. The Detroit Golf Club veteran exploded from the trap within seven feet of the pin on Red Run's first hole, the first playoff hole, and dropped the putt for a winning birdie" beating Bob Whiting and Gene Woodward.

Bob was always a great player out of the sand traps. Like I mentioned earlier, it seemed he did his best shots when he was in trouble, like in the sand or in the trees. My theory was that he not only thought about his shot more but he enjoyed the challenge of the obstacle.

Bob traveled to Columbus, Ohio late that August to play in the American-Italian Golf Association's Invitational Tournament. Go figure, Bob was Polish, not Italian. In a short newspaper clipping about that event published in The Columbus Citizen on August 27, 1956, it said, "Bob Babbish, 41-year-old Detroit steel salesman, who features 330-yard drives, slipped into town 'on business' over the weekend and made it his business to cop medalist honors among 110 contestants. Babbish, playing the hilly Bridgeview Country Club for the first time, clicked for seven birdies, slipped for four bogeys and bagged a three-under-par 68. He edged ex-Ohio Stater Johnny Zoller's 69 for the medal trophy for lowest score but Zoller got a fine seven-stroke meshing from his partner Rudy Biscoitti to win the AA best-ball division with 62, two strokes under Babbish and his partner Jake Nadalin."

You can see how "businessman golf" was working out for Bob in more ways than one. I am sure that his member partner was a steel customer that Bob's company wanted to do business with and Bob just happened to time his sales visit the week of the tournament and the customer just happened to belong to the club having it. And Bob's company paid for the trip as it was a business trip. He was an educated man!

Bob also won the Dearborn Country Club Invitational in 1956 for the second time in a row as well as the Grosse Isle Country Club Invitational that year. The Grosse Isle Country Club was Glenn Johnson's home club so that was a bit of revenge for Glenn beating him so often in 1955. That's Bob on the right in a photograph taken at this tournament on the next page.

# GROSSE ILE INVITATIONALS 20ᵀᴴ ANNIVERSARY 1956

In February 1957, Bob and Delphine had their second child, a girl they named Bernice Ann after both grandmothers. Bob was still working as a salesman for the steel company and was doing very well there and was pulling in a very good salary. Plus he could play golf up to seven months of the year entertaining customers at his office, the South Course of Detroit Golf Club. Weekends too were spent playing golf, at least in the mornings, a schedule that lasted for many many years.

Bob qualified for his eighth U.S. Open in 1957. All we know is that he had to withdraw for some reason before it happened, the first time he didn't play in it after qualifying

This golf schedule of Bob's came up in an article by John Walter appearing in the May 27th, 1957 edition of The Detroit News about Bob winning the Detroit Medal Play Tournament for the second year in a row. "Bob credits a little wifely 'advice' for his success in repeating as the Detroit Medal Play Champion. He matched par of 278 for the 72 holes in the third annual tournament completed yesterday at his home course, Detroit Golf Club. 'We have a new baby at our house' the four-time District champion related after being presented with the John J. Pomeroy Trophy. His daughter, Bernice, is three months old and he has a son, Byron, 3½ years. 'Things are just a little different,' he said, referring to feeding the baby, changing diapers, etc. which can play havoc with weekend rounds of golf. 'The word this morning was if I didn't win, I didn't get to play golf this weekend.' With the win Bob had his wife's permission to play in the Dearborn Invitational that next weekend." [Editor's note: I don't recall Bob ever feeding the baby or changing a diaper.]

A second article about this 1957 Detroit Medal Play Tournament was written by Tom McPhail in another Detroit paper. It was titled, "Babbish Starts Round Losing by 2 and Wins by 12." "Bob Babbish, a graying 41-year-old steel salesman, laughed at Sunday's snappish winds and a field of 29 other golfers while winning the Detroit Medal Play championship by 12 strokes with a 72-hole score of 278. Babbish matched par on Detroit Golf Club's South Course with a 68 and went one-over with a 73 on the north course in the afternoon. He started the day two strokes behind Ben Smith who finished second after a rough last two rounds. Babbish carded a pair of bogies and two birdies in the morning and came back with seven bogies and five birdies in the afternoon.

"He needed a little luck on the par-three seventh hole in the afternoon, however. His tee shot, a strong Number 1 iron, sailed over the green, hit a roadway marker stone and dropped back within 25 feet of the green. He chipped to the edge of the green and sank a 10-foot putt for par."

Free Press Photo by TOM VENALECK

A ROCKY RECOVERY of a seventh-hole tee shot saved Bob Babbish, defending Detroit Medal Play titlist, from at least a double bogey Sunday. His No. 1 iron tee shot sailed over the green, bound for a clump of trees, hit a roadway marker stone (foreground) and bounced to a stop. It left Babbish with an easy chip to the green and a 10-foot putt for a par three.

" 'If I hadn't hit that stone I would have had a double-bogey for sure,' he said. Most players said that they were troubled by the brisk winds, which bent tee shots and held back approaches although the confident Babbish seemed unaffected. 'When you're six strokes up, how can anything bother you?' he asked at the start of the final 18 holes."

Of interest in these articles was the reference Bob using a Number 1 iron. He always felt more comfortable with his iron game than his wood one. He would carry the additional Number 1 iron instead of a wood in his bag and use it quite often for most of his golf career. I remember him using a Number 1 iron as late as the mid-1970's.

In 1957 Bob was the low qualifier for the National Amateur Championship played at Brookline, Massachusetts. This turned out to be the last time he played in this tournament. The record does not show how he fared in it that year but I do have an article from The Detroit News by Lewis H. Walter about the qualification rounds held at the Country Club of Detroit. "Four first-timers are among the 10 Michigan area golfers who have qualified for the USGA Amateur championship at Brookline, Massachusetts on September 9-14. But Michigan's No. 1 qualifier is Bob Babbish of Detroit who has won a place in the field for the tenth time. Babbish topped a field of 65 at the Country Club with 71-75 for 146 yesterday. [Editor Note: Ten being a typo as it was seven.]

"The onetime U of D player, now a chubby and prematurely gray manufacturer's agent, fired four birdies on his morning round in which he was tied for the lead with Gerry Berles, 27, former Miami (Florida) University star from Grand Rapids. In the afternoon one birdie and a three-over par score was enough to get him home two strokes in front."

Also in 1957 Bob played in the Black River Country Club's Annual Invitational in Port Huron, Michigan with Bud Gould and led after the first round but lost in the final match 4 to 2 to the team of Neil Boyle and Joe Grace. The match reportedly featured spectacular long hitting by Babbish and Grace. Bob also won the Detroit Golf Club Spring Medal Play Tournament that year.

His friendship with Bud Gould not only meant teaming up with him for many tournaments but Bud also introduced Bob to the rich and famous in Detroit and the nation. Bud brought Bob into a level of high society that only golf could have taken him to.

Bud's influence on Bob was usually the result of using the status and resources of his company, Murray Corporation. Remember, Bob did not work for Murray Corporation, but as Bud's friend, Murray Corporation was happy to work for Bob. I bet Bob sold a lot of steel to Murray Corporation.

This was seen in January 1958 when Murray Corporation was the company that sponsored the Bing Crosby National Pro-Am Tournament's first time on national television. Bud was able to arrange for Bob to play in the tournament and flew Bob and Delphine out to California in the company plane.

Above is a shot of the Murray Corporation entourage boarding the company's DC-3 airplane at City Airport in Detroit for the trip to California to play in the Bing Crosby National Pro-Am in 1958.

Staying at the Del Monte Lodge at Pebble Beach golf club, Bob and Delphine rubbed elbows with the rich and famous. Bing invited many fellow celebrities to play and at the end of the tournament they all were invited to the famous *Victory Dinner and Clambake*, a copy of the invitation to it appearing below.

On the next pages are some photographs they took at the 1958 event showing the course and some celebrities.

Bob Hope and Fred Waring at the Del Monte Lodge in
1958 for the Bing Crosby tournament.

Bob's foursome for the 1958 Bing Crosby tournament.
Bob is on the left and the names of the others forgotten.

Bing Crosby giving an interview for the TV audience.

A shot of players in the tournament with the Pacific Ocean.

Bing teeing off on the water hole in front of the TV camera

Bob and Delphine relaxing at the Del Monte Lodge.

Bob Hope walking off a green at Pebble Beach in 1958.

Bob was also enjoying being a father of two at this time. Below is a photograph of him with my sister and me at the house on Muirland taken late in 1957.

The Detroit Golf Club, being just a mile away from his house on Muirland Street, was often the place for family fun as well as golfing. I remember a lavish Christmas Party held at the club in the late 1950's and the photographs on the next page are from that event. That is me in the top shot showing my skills to the crowd there with the latest fad back then, the "Hula-Hoop." Below that is my sister and me visiting with Santa who surprisingly appeared.

Below is a photograph taken of the whole Babbish family at my fourth birthday party held on Muirland in 1957 and of Bob taking the kids sledding at, where else, the Detroit Golf Club that same winter.

Here is a rare family shot taken at Detroit Golf Club in 1958 of, not Bob, but his protégé son doing some practice putting. Though I did play a lot of golf when young and even shot a 78 once, I couldn't beat Dad and gave up.

More shots taken at the Detroit Golf Club in 1958.

In 1959, the only tournament we know that Bob played in was again the Bing Crosby National Pro-Am in California. Bud Gould and Murray Corporation flew him and Delphine there in the company plane, as Murray was again the tournament's television sponsor. I remember staying at his bother John's house while they were gone.

Right after this tournament, Bob flew his young family down to Florida for a two-month vacation in the sun. How did this work? Well, Bud Gould had a winter house in Palm Beach and flew back and forth to it using the company plane. His wife Billie spent the winters there and he suggested to Bob that if we wanted to do the same he could hitch a ride with them on the plane. Bob took him up on this and down to Florida the Babbish family went on January 31, 1959. The way it worked was Delphine and the kids stayed at a beachside hotel in Miami Beach named the *Golden Falcon* for two months and Bob and Bud would fly down in the company plane every weekend. Below we are boarding the new Murray Corp. Convair airplane in Detroit.

Bob and his kids on the plane ride to Florida in 1959. The cabin was not pressurized on the new Convair airplane Murray Corporation bought that year and I remember my ears bothering me the whole flight.

Bob rented a car for the entire stay (a 1959 Oldsmobile convertible) and came down every weekend as planned. We had a great time in Florida that winter. It was before I was in school so we were not missing anything but a Michigan winter. We did all the tourist sites and went out to eat all the time. I remember swimming in the ocean. We had one bad hurricane-like storm while we were there and afterwards the beach was covered with "Man 'O War" jellyfish. One day coming back from dinner I looked in the sky and saw something I never saw before nor had many others. A rocket had just lifted off from Cape Canaveral as part of the early space program and we could see the flame of the rocket arching into the sky in the early evening dusk.

Our rented 1959 Oldsmobile convertible in Miami Beach, Florida in 1959, compliments of Zip Ellis.

Another story about Bob's Businessman Golf years of the late 1950's relates to his business trips to New York. His steel company used to purchase a lot of its steel that it sold in Detroit from Bethlehem Steel Corporation. Bob often had to travel to New York City to Bethlehem Steel's offices there and, of course, there was more to it than just business.

Bob said that on a Thursday night he and Sol Eisenberg, the owner of his steel company, and other company executives would board the New York Central train *Detroiter* in Detroit for the overnight trip to New York City. He recalled that since the first four hours of the trip was through Canada he had to pre-order his liquor drinks before the train left the station in Detroit due to customs regulations. He had a berth on the train but he said he never used it as he and his boss and others going on the trip would spend the night playing cards in the observation car lounge at the rear of the train.

Upon arriving in New York City the next morning, a limousine from Bethlehem Steel would pick them up at Grand Central Station and take them to their 10 am meeting with the Bethlehem Steel sales staff on Park Avenue. There they would conduct some business, break for a long lunch at a nice restaurant, conduct some more business, then get back into the limousine by mid-afternoon (to avoid rush hour traffic) for the two-hour drive to headquarters at Bethlehem, PA.

At Bethlehem they would meet with other executives of the company and go out for a big dinner lasting way into the evening. Come Saturday everyone from dinner met at the local private golf club and played 36 holes of golf, have another big dinner lasting way into the evening, then they would wake up Sunday for another 18 holes of golf. After the golf game on Sunday they got a ride in the limo back to Grand Central Station to take the overnight train *Empire State Express* back to Detroit. Bob said that Sol always let him have Monday off of work after these hectic "business" trips. You can bet these were largely organized because of Bob's fame as a golfer. Those certainly were the "good 'ole days" of business.

Bob at one of the Bethlehem Steel "business meetings" in New York City in the late 1950's celebrating a big purchase of steel and a job well done. Now for the golfing part.

Another story about Bob and a golfing event with the rich and famous was that in the late 1950's Bud Gould arranged for him and his wife along with Bob and Delphine to fly to Augusta National Golf Club in Georgia to play golf one weekend. Of course, they took the Murray Corporation plane there. The weekend was prearranged well in advance. On the plane's approach to the local airport, the pilot was told to take a holding pattern. This was odd as there was little if any airplane traffic in and out of that airport. Once they were cleared for landing the control tower explained that they were held so President Eisenhower's plane could land.

To make things even more interesting, when Bob's party arrived at the golf course it was empty. Turns out that no one could enter the clubhouse or play golf that weekend as President Eisenhower and his wife Mamie were visiting there. Somehow Bud's reservation was honored and the four of them shared the entire club that weekend with the President, Mamie, secret service and host Bobby Jones, the famous golfer and owner of the course.

Bob would tell stories of his foursome playing golf behind the President's that weekend and that Ike was very slow and a poor player. "Not like you could yell up that you wanted to play through that day" Bob would say. They sat at the table next to the President and his wife at dinner at the clubhouse each night that weekend. The President and Mamie stayed in one of the famous small cabins lining the course like Bob and Delphine did and they were neighbors. Bob said that when he wasn't playing golf, Ike would be outside the cabin painting, one of his pastimes. As you know, he painted the famous portrait of Bobby Jones that still is hanging in the clubhouse. Bob owned a print of this painting and it is hanging in my house now.

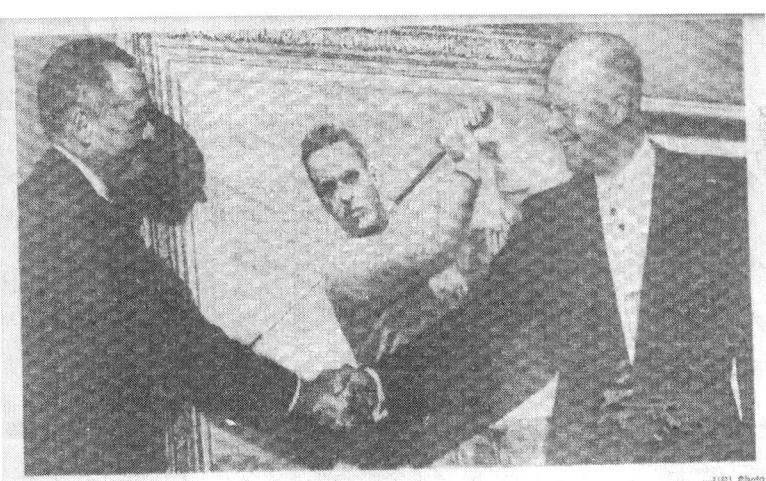

—UPI Photo

ARTIST'S GIFT—Bobby Jones shakes hands with the late President Dwight D. Eisenhower after Mr. Eisenhower had presented Jones with this portrait of the golfer, which the President had painted. The presentation was made Feb. 28, 1953, at the Augusta National Golf Course at Atlanta shortly after Mr. Eisenhower's first inauguration.

Bob in the 1950's with his score plaque at a tournament.
The plaque says that Bob is out of Royal Oak so it must
have been from a 1950 tournament while he was still a
member at Red Run Golf Club.

As you can see, the decade of the 1950's was a great one for Bob. Golf, work and family all came together and life was very good. The American Dream at its best, all because of an athletic talent, college education and great personality. Bob's greatest decision was to be a businessman golfer for as much as he liked to golf, he never would have made so much money and had such a comfortable lifestyle and still played so much golf if he had turned professional. From talking to him, the thought of turning pro never entered his mind, not even when he was The Great Babbish in the 1930's. "No money in it until the 1960's when the tournaments were televised" he once told me, "and I was too old come 1960 to have been able to take advantage of it." He said that a number of his friends who turned pro did so by accident, usually by accepting prize money under the table or something, and getting caught by the golf association. That was an automatic conversion to professional status. His friends Chick Harbert and Bob Gajda accidently turned pro that way.

Miscellaneous photographs taken from this decade follow to finish up this chapter. These are shots where the location, date and often the people in them are no longer known but can be placed as taken in the 1950's, largely by how gray Bob's hair was getting. By the 1960's, his hair had prematurely turned all gray. Other than in photographs, I do not recall Bob with much if any black hair. He kept all his gray, then white, hair until he died.

Bob and Bud Gould at some tournament award ceremony. Not sure which tournament it was or the significance of the Lady Bing Trophy being presented to Bob by Bud but, by the looks of that tall trophy on the table, it was a big one.

Another mystery photo, date and location but that's Chuck Kocsis second from left and Bob at far right.

**Bob Babbish and Ben Smith**
*Three-Time District Champions*

This must have been taken in 1953 as Bob won the District Championship for a third time that year and Ben had won it the previous year.

Another 1950's photograph with Bob on the far left and Chuck Kocsis on the far right at a location and event lost to memory, as are the names of the other two golfers.

This one might have been taken at Shawnee Golf Resort.

# CHAPTER 9
## SUBURBAN LIFE AND CLUB GOLF: 1960 TO 1981

The decade of the 1960's marked, except for one last time, the end of Bob participating in national or state golf tournaments. But this did not end his golfing or playing in tournaments. He remained active in local golf club championships and invitational tournaments and would remain so for the next thirty years.

In 1960 Bob played in his last Michigan Medal Play Championship. He had won this five-year old tournament twice, in 1956 and 1957. Chuck Kocsis had won it the other three times. An article on the 1960 Championship in the Detroit Times newspaper dated May 15, 1960 written by Ron Smith had the headline, " State Medal Play Battle Cry: 'Beat Kocsis, Beat Babbish.' "

The article began, "Detroit's first major golf tournament of 1960 – the Michigan Medal Play Championship – starts Friday at Western Golf and Country Club [in Redford]. Most of the district's best amateurs and several from outstate will converge on the exacting, rugged course with two objectives: 1 – Shoot better than Chuck Kocsis, 2 – Shoot better than Bob Babbish. This will probably win the tournament. But it will take some doing. Kocsis and Babbish are the only men who have won the Medal Play.

"Babbish and Kocsis will not lack for competition. Top threat to the two-way stranglehold on the championship is Melvin (Bud) Stevens, the District and State Amateur champion [both in 1959] who makes Western his home course. Stevens knows the Western's layout well."

All we know is that Bob did not win the Michigan Medal Play Tournament in 1960.

INCLUDE ME—Melvin (Bud) Stevens didn't say that as he walked in on Chuck Kocsis and Bob Babbish talking over old times, but it could work out that way in the sixth annual Michigan Medal Play championship at Western Golf Club May 20-22. Stevens is district and state amateur champ while Kocsis won the medal play event three times and Babbish took the honors twice.

Detroit Times Photo by Edward C. Nole

230

Bob had been a member of the Detroit Golf Club since 1951 and in most years he played in their annual club championship. We know that he won it in 1954 then again in 1960 and 1962.

In Bob's personal life, the new decade started out with him still being the sales manager for the steel company. He must have been making good money because in 1960 he had a custom-built home constructed in Bloomfield Township, just kitty corner from the North Course of Oakland Hills Country Club.

At this time the suburbs of Detroit were just starting to become developed. Up to then, most of them were just farmland or small towns. No one moved out there from the big city back then yet. Why Bob wanted to move from his beloved Detroit north ten miles into the suburbs is lost to memory. It was probably the up and coming thing to do at the time and Bob would have been a trendsetter or pathfinder. It was prophetic and timely as within seven years the great exodus out of Detroit to the suburbs started, largely because of the 1967 Detroit Riots.

The move was orchestrated by a friend of Bob's, Howard Keating. Howard was a golf buddy and was one of the original developers in the suburbs at that time. He had purchased an old horse farm in Bloomfield Township to develop into a suburban neighborhood and sold one of the first lots to Bob to build his dream house on.

During this age of suburban construction in Detroit's surrounding regions great home builders like Pulte got started. Many of the homes in Bob's new neighborhood were built by Pulte, some of the first ones Pulte did. Bob hired a custom homebuilder, Fortnier Bros., to design and build his house. Construction of it started during the winter of 1959/60. Bob took the family out there on many trips to "supervise" the construction.

The basement of 3514 Darcy Drive is dug and the
construction of the house has begun in late 1959. That's
Bob and the author inspecting the progress in both of the
photographs. I still have the blueprints for the house.

Two shots showing the progress of the new house on
Darcy Drive during the winter of 59/60. Top photo is Bob
and his brother John and sister-in-law Esther and Bob's
1959 Chevy and below is Bob, in black, his brother-in-law
Mike Mikula and the author with Del's 1960 Oldsmobile.

The route from Bob's house on Muirland to Bloomfield Township to visit the new house under construction was taking Northwestern Highway to Lahser Road then north on Lahser six miles. At that intersection there was a rural Shell gas station that Bob would always stop at, not only to get gas but also to give his kids a treat and a taste of what was to be in store for them at their new house. Behind the gas station was a small horse farm and the family who lived there gave out pony rides to people. For all I know, that family also owned the gas station too. After the horseback ride (and probably a bathroom break too, as it was a long ride back then before expressways) it was off to visit the new house being built and to see what changes had occurred since the last visit.

The routine on those weekend drives to visit the new house being built in the suburbs always included a stop for gas and a quick pony ride at the corner of Northwestern Highway and Lahser Road in Southfield, as seen above. The author is riding the horse with one of the owner's kids.

Bob and his family moved into the new house on Darcy Drive in the summer of 1960. It was the fourth house in the new subdivision that eventually had 40 houses in it. Delphine never forgave Bob and never let him or anyone forget that on moving day Bob was playing golf instead of helping. I always thought what was the big deal? That it was a smart move by Bob.

In the photo above it is moving day for Bob and his family to the new house on Darcy Drive in June 1960. Notice no lawn or even driveway yet (the moving van just backed up the front yard to the front door), the dirt road in the foreground and one of the three other houses next door.

For me as a seven-year-old who grew up in the city, I was moving to the country. We had pheasants, quails, a "forest" in the form of a wood lot on the south side of the neighborhood with a stream and a horse field on the north side along our house with two horses and a barn on it. I "inspected" and played in each of the other 36 homes

A shot of Rusty (left) and Doc (right), the horses from the horse farm behind Bob's house on Darcy in a photograph taken before moving into the new house. The farmhouse of Mr. Maxwell can be seen in the background on the hill.

built in the neighborhood after we moved in, knowing more about them than their owners ever did. We fed the horses through the split rail fence out back on our border with the farm. We climbed trees and built tree forts, learned the birds and animals (something I still enjoy today), built dams on a stream running through the woodlot and got to know all the new neighbors and their many children. It was the greatest area to grow up and certainly the best time as life was innocent and you didn't lock your doors or worry where your children were or what they were doing. Dad would just give his loud finger-whistle from the front door when it was dinnertime to come home and I would do so.

It is the summer of 1960 and Bob and his family are all moved into his new house and the driveway is in (but the road is still dirt). Now it was time to landscape it and the first step of that was laying sod for the grass as seen above with the sod truck in front of the house.

One funny story from the early days living on Darcy Drive came right after the sod was laid on the lawn. The lawn looked great. It made the yard look like an oasis in a field of dirt and weeds that the neighborhood still was. The next morning I was awakened by Bob yelling out the back door at something. I ran downstairs and could see that our beautiful new sod lawn looked like bombs had been dropped on it. Large rectangular sections were torn up throughout the back yard. Then I saw what Bob was yelling at.

Both of the horses, their names were Doc and Rusty, had found a way through the split rail fence along the horse farm border and were enjoying a nice tasty buffet breakfast of Kentucky Blue Grass, compliments of the new neighbors! And no yelling by some old man in the house was going to scare them away from this unexpected feast.

After the shock of seeing what was happening to our new lawn, Bob made the long walk to Mr. Maxwell's house, the owner of the horses, introduced himself as his new and unhappy neighbor and told him what his horses were up to. Mr. Maxwell came over and got his two horses and walked them back to the barn. We spent the rest of the day relaying our sod. Later that summer I met Mr. Maxwell again as he and his sons were putting in a barbed wire fence along his entire property line a few feet inside the split rail fence to keep the horses inside.

To me, this was the greatest event that ever happened yet in my short six years of life. Real live horses in our backyard. What a great place this new house and neighborhood was and how exciting to have horses in your backyard! And Bob handled the situation so well. I still remember the sight of Doc and Rusty being led by Mr. Maxwell up Darcy Drive to Lahser Road so he could get them back in the barn. It was like living in the Wild West.

Looking out back from Bob's home at the horses and field.

There were a lot of teenage girls that eventually moved into the neighborhood as it was quickly filling up with families. They all loved the two horses on the farm out back and wanted to ride them. At some point they focused on a large tree in the horse field that had a big drooping limb. A girl would climb on that limb and another would guide a saddle-less horse underneath it so the girl on the limb could plop on the horse's back and ride it bareback in the field. Old Doc and Rusty never minded the attention though eventually Mr. Maxwell found out and stopped it.

There was another neighborhood girl the same age and grade as I was who lived four houses up the street from me. She grew up in the suburbs so this life outside of the city was all she knew. I remember many times she and I would argue about what we called our area. I insisted we lived out in the "country" as we had horses and wildlife and barns and fields and space. She would argue back that no, we lived in the "suburbs," and that the country was further north of us. For a city boy like I was, we lived in the country.

Living in the suburbs gave Bob the opportunity to do things that he never did growing up in the city. Remember that Bob spent his first five years on the farm in Pennsylvania so he did have a country background. This came out with the way he wasn't afraid of Doc and Rusty, the horses out back, rescuing mice in the basement sink that couldn't get out, the making of fires in the fireplace in the family room in the winter, etc.

There was a good-sized lake about a half-mile away named Gilbert Lake and, as mentioned earlier, that first winter on Darcy Bob took me there and taught me to ice skate. I was amazed that Bob knew how to, it just didn't seem something he would know. But he was a great skater and quickly had me skating on that frozen lake. Years later

I read that article in the newspaper that mentioned Bob was a star hockey player at Pershing High School and almost pursued hockey instead of golf. Yes, he knew how to skate even though he was a city boy.

I mentioned that Oakland Hills Country Club wasn't too far away from the house on Darcy. The northeast corner of the North Course of Oakland Hills, which was a public course back then, was almost at the southwest corner of our neighborhood. I always wondered why Bob didn't buy a lot in the new neighborhood along the North Course there as it was being developed the same time our neighborhood was and Bob, as you know, played golf. Anyway, during the winters when we first lived there Bob would take me to the North Course (no fences back then), which was very hilly, and go sledding. The hills were huge to me and we had a great time sledding there.

There were also a small pond in that northeast corner of the North Course and we went skating there too. Later when I was a bit older and more independent the neighborhood boys would get together and drag our sticks, skates, shovels and even the hockey nets we made (that could be folded up for travel) on sleds to this pond, shovel it off, and play hockey on it all day long on Saturdays in the winter thanks to Bob teaching me how to skate.

One time in these early years on Darcy Bob told me to get my clubs (of course I had a small set of cut-down clubs that his club-making friend Stan Sabbit of Gorman Golf made for me) and he and I walked over to the North Course and played on it starting at the hole in the northeast corner. I didn't think much of this, as there was no one else playing, but years later when I used to do this myself I realized we had sneaked on it without paying. Bob later said that Al Watrous, the professional at Oakland Hills, and he were good friends from way back and he had Al's permission to do so. For years friends and I would do the same thing, never paying for a round, based on the assumption that Mr. Watrous wouldn't mind. Eventually Oakland Hills made the North Course private so they had a 36-hole golf club. That ended the hockey, sledding and golfing there as soon a fence went up to keep the riffraff like us out.

Bob always got me a couple tickets to the many PGA and USGA tournaments held at Oakland Hills in the 1960's. I remember seeing Arnold Palmer, Jack Nicholas, Gary Player, Lee Travino, Chi Chi Rodriquez and all the great golfers from that era play there up close. Chi Chi once even gave me and friend Bill Potter a golf ball while we were watching him tee up on a hole during a tournament. Bob never went to any of these, though.

Bob used to take us on trips out to the country from our suburban house. These were trips to Franklin Cider Mill (which is still there) or to some place where we could ride horses. These horse riding trips were usually out in Troy or Sterling Heights, two areas that developed later than our area and remained rural farmland for another ten years. Bob loved to visit the many mushroom farms that dotted Sterling Heights back then. These were usually dark, dirty concrete block bunker-like buildings that smelled of horse manure, which was used to fertilize the mushrooms that grew inside the windowless building in the dark. Sometimes the owner would give us all a miner's hardhat with a flashlight attached to it and we would go inside the bowels (appropriate word for it from the way it smelled with the manure being the dirt) of the mushroom farm and pick our own mushrooms. No wonder why I never ate mushrooms until much later in life.

A shot taken from one of the trips out to the farmlands of Troy and Sterling Heights and sneaking in a little horseback riding while doing so back in the 1960's. That is one of Bob's Buick company cars on the right.

While Bob worked for the steel company he had a new company car every year or so. Delphine first had that 1955 Chevy and then a sharp 1960 Oldsmobile that is on Page 233 in front of the new house, then a 1962 Plymouth convertible that she kept until 1967. Dad was driving a new Buick each year, usually a La Sabre four-door model. I must have developed my interest and love for cars from Bob's company cars as I always wanted to know all about them and went through them all the first day he brought a new one home.

It was also very neat that we had a garage. Bob's house on Muirland in Detroit did not have a garage and now he had one that was part of the house. Bob always appreciated keeping his car in it as it was the first time he didn't have to keep a car outside in the elements, especially during winter with the snow and cold.

As Bob now lived out in the country, I mean suburbs, there wasn't the convenience of local stores to shop at like there was in the city. These eventually were built but for the first few years we had to drive a pretty good distance to do our shopping. One location that was about halfway between Bob's old house on Muirland and the new one on Darcy Drive was Northland Center Mall. Opened just a few years earlier in 1954, it was the first large suburban retail-shopping center in Detroit and one of the first in the nation. Bob would often take the family there to shop.

Northland Center Mall, in the background, as seen from the Reynolds Aluminum Building across Northwestern Highway, which was designed by Minoru Yamasaki.

Playing on the statutes by the famous local sculptor
Marshall Fredericks that dotted the grounds of the
Northland Center Mall in the early 1960's. Back then this
mall was all open instead of enclosed like today's malls are
and was like visiting a small town's shopping area.

After Bob moved to Darcy Drive I remember him
taking the family on long driving trips every other weekend
or so during the summer to visit his mother Anna at her
"cottage" in New Baltimore on Anchor Bay off of Lake St.
Clair. I later found out that Anna and some of Bob's
brothers had built this small home out in the country on

the lake for Anna and her fourth husband, Joe Palinski. I am not sure when it was built but the first time I remember Bob taking us there was after we moved to Darcy in 1960.

It was a long, country drive to the cottage, taking east/west roads and north/south roads to angle our way northeast. There were no expressways back then in our area. We would usually stop at some farm along the way and buy corn and other fresh produce from the roadside stand. Bob loved fresh vegetables. Sometimes we stopped at a mushroom farm. Usually there were many aunts and uncles and cousins at the cottage every time we went. It would be "pot-luck" and there was plenty of food to eat. It gave me a chance to really get to know them all.

An early shot at Anna's cottage in New Baltimore. Brothers Walter and Frank, sister-in-law Cecil and wife Delphine on the left and mother Anna on the right.

Of course there was also the allure of getting a boat ride on Anchor Bay those visits. Brother John would usually be the skipper on the classy Chris Craft wooden boat that Anna owned and we would sail out of the dock on the canal the cottage was on and make our way out to the open sea, or so it seemed to me, for a fabulous and usually high-speed boat ride on Anchor Bay.

Anna in her very large vegetable garden at the cottage in New Baltimore in 1964. Her house is the one on the right. She also went fishing for perch in Anchor Bay and was almost self-sufficient when it came to food there. She is holding her beloved and long-lived poodle, Tiger.

The move to the suburbs was a great one for Bob and his family. They lived in that house until 1984 when they moved full-time to Florida. They sold it to a college classmate of mine who I see a couple of times a year and who keeps me informed of all the old neighborhood news. Of course, the drive to the Detroit Golf Club was a lot longer now than before but that didn't affect how often

Bob played.

Getting back to the topic of golf, all of Bob's golf now was with customers during the week and with friends on weekends. Yes, he played golf every day of the week except Monday when the club was closed for maintenance. Bob, a devout Catholic, said that the greatest thing the Church ever did for him was, in the post-Vatican II days of the late 1960's, to allow the obligatory Sunday Mass to be held on Saturday evenings. This freed up Sunday mornings for an early golf game now so maybe he could sneak a second round in on Sunday afternoons.

In addition to leisure and business golf, Bob did play in many of the Detroit Golf Club tournaments during this period as well as a few other club's invitational's where he was invited by a member to play with. The record indicates that he won at least one of these invitationals in the 1960's, the Pine Lake Country Club Invitational in 1963. I remember this one as Bob took us to the awards ceremony at Pine Lake and allowed my sister and me to pick out the two prizes he was entitled to at the table where all the prizes were. I picked a set of binoculars in a leather case (which I still have) and my sister picked a bicycle, her first one. Bob won the Detroit Golf Club Championship in 1960 and 1962 as was mentioned above. He played in this tournament almost every year until he moved to Florida and was always a contender.

When Bob reached age 55 in 1970 he also played in the Detroit Golf Club Senior Club Championship. He won the Seniors there in 1973, 1974, 1975, 1980 and in 1981 at which time he was 66 years old. On the next pages are two photographs taken during the 1965 Detroit Golf Club Championship. The first one shows the famous Babbish "Jump" when he hit a tee shot with the driver and the other one is with his friend Ben Smith who won that year.

In the early 1960's, Bob had a falling out with his boss at the steel company and quit. He started up his own business, representing other manufacturers that used steel products, and did this until the mid-1970's. This didn't work out as well money-wise and so his wife went back to work teaching, something she did until they both retired in 1981.

In the mid-1970's, Bob had a couple rough years with his business and got depressed about it. Delphine arranged for me, at that time a college student back home for the summer, to meet with Bob's old friend and former boss, Sol Eisenberg, to see if Sol could find Bob a job at his steel company again. Bob was unaware of this meeting and wouldn't have allowed it if he knew. I didn't want to do it either as I didn't expect any results because as far as I knew Bob and Sol were still not getting along.

I contacted Sol and he arranged to meet me at the Knollwood Country Club in West Bloomfield Township where he was a long-time member. We met in the dining room for lunch. I still remember reintroducing myself (I presumed we had met when I was young but that was years ago) and then asking him, "How is business?" His reply to me was a lesson I will never forget: "We are here to talk about friendships, not business." I will also never forget what Sol said next, just when I was ready to bring up the "topic" I was there for but never had a chance to. He said right off that he had arranged to hire Bob back as a salesman if he wanted to come back. Everything was all set and he was going to have his sales manager contact him so as not to give it away that Sol was behind it. And that was that. Sol knew exactly what I was there for, must have admired me for having the courage to help Bob out (I didn't tell him Delphine had sent me) and I didn't even have to ask. The rest of the meeting was all social.

Sol was a class act. Bob started working there that year and stayed there until he retired in 1981. He soon got a company car (it was a 1977 Chevy Caprice, a redesigned model for that year) and got over his depression. Plus the company was paying his Detroit Golf Club dues and expenses and encouraging Bob to take his customers out to golf just like in the old days. It worked out great.

A photograph from the awards ceremony of the 1974 Birmingham Country Club Invitational. Bob, second from the right, obviously did not win as he is not holding the trophy but must have placed. Tommy Sheehan is to Bob's right, Ben Smith to his left and Glenn Johnson the third from the left. The names of the others are not remembered.

Two more club championship shots taken at unknown
locations in the 1960's or 1970's, Bob second to the
left on top and on the right on the bottom
with other unrecalled players.

In 1979 Bob was inducted to the Michigan Amateur Sports Hall of Fame. I remember the ceremony as I attended it. It was in some hall in Detroit and the famous Detroit radio celebrity, J. P, McCarthy, was Bob's sponsor and was going to give Bob's introduction and a little speech about him. Bob's golf introduced him to all the local Detroit celebrities as they all wanted to play with him. He was friends with Gordie Howe, Sid Able and Ted Lindsay of Detroit Red Wing hockey team's "Production Line" fame, Al Kaline of the Detroit Tigers, the famous lawyer William Henry Gallagher who took on Henry Ford and won, Max Fisher, the industrialist and philanthropist that all Presidents since FDR called for advice, and many others.

Anyway, good ole' J.P. didn't show for the event and sent his assistant to fill in for him, who, by the way, gave a very nice speech. Below is the plaque presented to Bob at that ceremony.

**ROBERT N. BABBISH**
GOLF
BORN JUNE 6, 1915

Michigan Open Amateur Champion, 1934 and 1937
Michigan Amateur Champion, 1935
Michigan Open Runner-Up, 1937
Western Amateur Champion, 1938, the only Michigan golfer to win this title.
Semi-Finalist in National Collegiate, 1938
Detroit District Amateur Champion 1940, 1950, 1953 and 1954
Low Amateur of the Detroit Motor City Open, 1950
Michigan Medalist Champion 1956 and 1957
Qualified for the National Amateur 7 times and played 5 times
Qualified for National Open 7 times and played 7 times
Has three Holes-in-One.

INDUCTED OCTOBER 9, 1979

One last Detroit Golf Club story before we end this chapter.  In the late 1970's a group of members led by Bob, all who played golf early on Sunday mornings with each other (thank goodness for Vatican II), decided to make their weekly game a little more formal.  They decided to call their Sunday event "The Hamtramck Open," named after the nearby Polish town that stayed a separate city during Detroit's expansion at the beginning of the century.  Many of the members were of Polish descent, including Bob.  They organized tee times on Sunday starting at 7 am when the club opened, kept a scoreboard and always played the shorter South Course (which back then Bob held the record on, a 61 for the par 68 course)

In addition, they had a lunch buffet catered by the club in a conference room upstairs afterwards, complete with gallons of liquor (someone at the club was overlooking the restriction on alcohol sales before noon on Sundays back then).  There was an entrance fee each Sunday that was used to pay for the food and drinks and prize money.

The funny thing was that the year The Hamtramck Open was first played one of the South Course's holes was torn up to try out a new kind of fescue grass.  So in its first year The Hamtramck Open was subtitled "The 17-Hole Golf Classic."  The Hamtramck Open even ended the golf season each year with a huge evening banquet held in the Club's dining room, where even more food and liquor was consumed.  As word got out about this event (probably because of the early Sunday liquor being served afterwards) more and more members started showing up each Sunday morning.  By its second year it had become a huge event.  They even had wait staff and a bartender at the buffet afterwards to handle all the people.  I often played golf in it.  What with my high handicap and the great golf I played one particular day (including an eagle on one hole that resulted in a technical hole-in-one with my handicap), I even won The Hamtramck Open one Saturday and got a share of the entrance fees as my winnings (did that make me a professional golfer, I wonder?).

Well, as you can guess, things were getting a bit out of hand after a couple years. The Hamtramck Open participants were outnumbering those playing in other Detroit Golf Club events, husbands (only men were allowed to play in it back in those pre-women's liberation days) were coming home drunk at noon on Sundays or not at all, some members didn't feel welcome to play in it though it was open to all, and maybe someone got wise to the liquor sales on Sunday morning problem. Anyway, after a few years the club management (though I remember the club manager playing in it most Sundays) shut down The Hamtramck Open, saying it was an illegal club within a club. The party was over but what a party it was.

Bob, center laughing, on a radio show in the 1930's.

# CHAPTER 10
## RETIREMENT IN FLORIDA: 1981 TO 2012

In 1981, Bob was 66 years old and his wife was 60. Delphine was able to retire from her teaching job that year with full benefits so both Bob and her retired together. The first thing they did was rent a condominium in Florida and they spent the winter of 1981/82 down south, something they always wanted to do.

Well, at least that was what Bob always wanted to do. Delphine was a bit reluctant to leave Michigan, even just for the winter, but Bob convinced her otherwise and found a wonderful place at the Meadows Resort in Sarasota. They knew a number of ex-Detroiters living at the Resort, which helped. Delphine once said that she fell in love with the place the moment they turned onto the Resort's road and took the long, winding drive through it to their condo. It was beautiful to her and she was sold. Good job Bob. I had had my doubts about it working out but was wrong.

Bob also really poured it on that first couple of years of retirement, taking Delphine to McDonalds every morning for coffee, among other things. Though shocked at his behavior, she accepted it and toughed it out. Many years later she said moving to Florida was the best thing she ever did. They lived there longer than they had on Darcy Drive.

After three years as "snowbirds," driving down to spend the winters in Florida then returning to their home in Michigan, they took the plunge and sold their house of 24 years on Darcy Drive and bought a place of their own at the Meadows Resort. Bob was now a member there after being a member at Detroit Golf Club for 33 years. They had a great "retirement" party at the Detroit Golf Club for him that I was fortunate enough to attend. Many of his old friends, members or not, were there to send Bob off to Florida for good. Below are photos from that party.

Top are all the attendees of the DGC retirement party for Bob (don't recall why the watermelon) and with Ben Smith.

Bob quickly became involved in the golf scene at The Meadows and in Sarasota. He was also very involved in playing bridge there, a hobby he developed in his 50's when his back was bothering him and interfering with his golf for a bit. There are always a lot of bridge players at golf clubs for some reason.

His wife Delphine even "threatened" to take up golf again now that they were both retired (she had played a bit when they were first married before she came to accept that she was a "golf widow") but only played a couple of times with him before retiring from it again once and for all. Apparently Bob had warned her of all the snakes and alligators roaming the Florida golf courses, which scared her (remember, Bob was an "educated" man).

Bob played in a number of senior golf tournaments in Florida, winning a few of them. One that I remember was where Bob was tied with another player after regulation play and then lost in the playoffs. When I asked him about it he said that he just got tired and his opponent was a young whipper-snapper who didn't. When I mentioned it was a senior's tournament and everyone was old who was playing in it, Bob replied that he was 72 years old and the other guy was only 50, having just turned the minimum age to play in the senior tournament. Bob did win the Florida Senior Medal Play Championship in 1989 when he was 74 years old, the last statewide tournament he played in.

Bob not only had a lot of former Detroit friends in Sarasota but also, with his personality and golf talent, made a lot of new friends there. Over the years he outlived not only all his brothers and sister but also most of his Detroit friends. When he used to come back to Detroit to visit once a year in the summer after retiring he would make golf games with all his old friends while up there. As the years went by he played less golf on these trips. Eventually the playing stopped and I asked him why. He said all his Detroit friends were either retired and living in Florida now or have died. Life goes on.

In 1989 Bob was inducted into the Michigan Golf Hall of Fame. This ceremony was held at Indianwood Golf Club in Lake Orion, Michigan. He and his wife flew back to Michigan for it. I remember the ceremony. This was a real honor as the Hall of Fame included professional golfers as well as Amateurs. Prior to this the two other Halls of Fame were just for Amateurs. Below is the painting they did of Bob for it, his only formal painting. He was 74 years old at the time.

When he moved to Florida full time in 1984 Bob sold one of their two cars and bought a golf cart instead. Bob played out of that golf cart until he stopped playing golf, it being the best vehicle he ever purchased according to him.

As he got older he needed more help from the other members of his foursome on the course. And they were more than willing to help The Great Babbish. It was like he had three caddies with him, helping Bob out of the cart, teeing up his ball on the tees, picking it up out of the hole (if they even let him putt at all instead of giving him a "gimmie"), finding it on the rough, picking him up if he fell down with too big of a Babbish Jump off the tee, etc. His long game shortened up but his short game remained great. Remember, he was the master with the irons and that wasn't as affected by old age.

When he reached 90 years-old Bob was down to playing golf only a couple times a week and was driving his cart to the clubhouse to play bridge the other days, a less tiring sport.

Bob played golf until he was 94 years old. That year he had fallen at home (not playing golf) and unknown to him at the time that fall caused a small "bleeder" in his skull that eventually landed him in the hospital for surgery to relieve the pressure. He never fully recovered from that surgery though he sure tried, getting back to walking on his own with a walker then a cane. He did stop playing golf, driving a car and driving the golf cart, though. During his recovery I once took him around in the golf cart, letting him drive to see if he felt comfortable doing so (he wasn't). We did stop at a putting green out where no one was playing and out of sight. I helped him onto the green and he putted balls for about an hour, doing rather well considering. But that turned out to be the last time he played golf.

Bob in a tournament in Florida in 1986 at age 71.

Unbeknownst to me at that time of hopeful optimism for his recovery, that day on the practice putting green I witnessed the last golf ball ever struck by The Great Babbish. I remember it went into the hole, the only one of the many putts he hit that day. And when it did Bob said, "Well, finally made one. As good a time as any to stop." That was in 2010. I figured "stop" meant for the day but it turned out to be forever.

How many golf balls had Bob hit over those past 83 years ending with that one? Even when he hit that last putt Bob had that same fierce concentration in his eyes as I am sure he had when he made that putt to win the Western Amateur in 1938 as he lined it up, stroked it and watched it roll towards the hole. He had that same look of victory as he had in 1938 and every time when the ball went into the cup with that always-satisfying hollow clunk. Every shot was the most important one yet for Bob. The passion for this game of golf never died until Bob did.

In September 2011 Bob had a stroke that sent him to a nursing home. He never got out of bed on his own again though he was still lucent and sharp of the mind. In January 2012 he had another stroke that left him unconscious and he never woke up from it. He passed away peacefully on January 24, 2012 at the ripe old age of 96. I was convinced he was going to live to be 100 but he did good enough. He outlived all his parents and siblings by age (Anna died at 92 and John at 93) and all his old friends from Detroit. His wife Delphine lived another three years before passing. Bob is buried back in Detroit, the city he loved that gave him so many opportunities to become the great man he was.

So this is the life story of my dad, Bob Babbish. It is the story of the American Dream for a boy born poor, the son of a coal miner in Pennsylvania, who, by opportunity, personality and a talent for the game of golf, made a great life for himself and his family and touched the lives of so many people during his 96 years. Everyone who met him loved him. And the world he lived through for almost a century: From horse-drawn carriages and candles for lighting, through two world wars, the Great Depression, man landing on the moon and the computer age (which he never used, couldn't see the use of one), Bob live through the greatest time in history and made it a great time in history for everyone he touched.

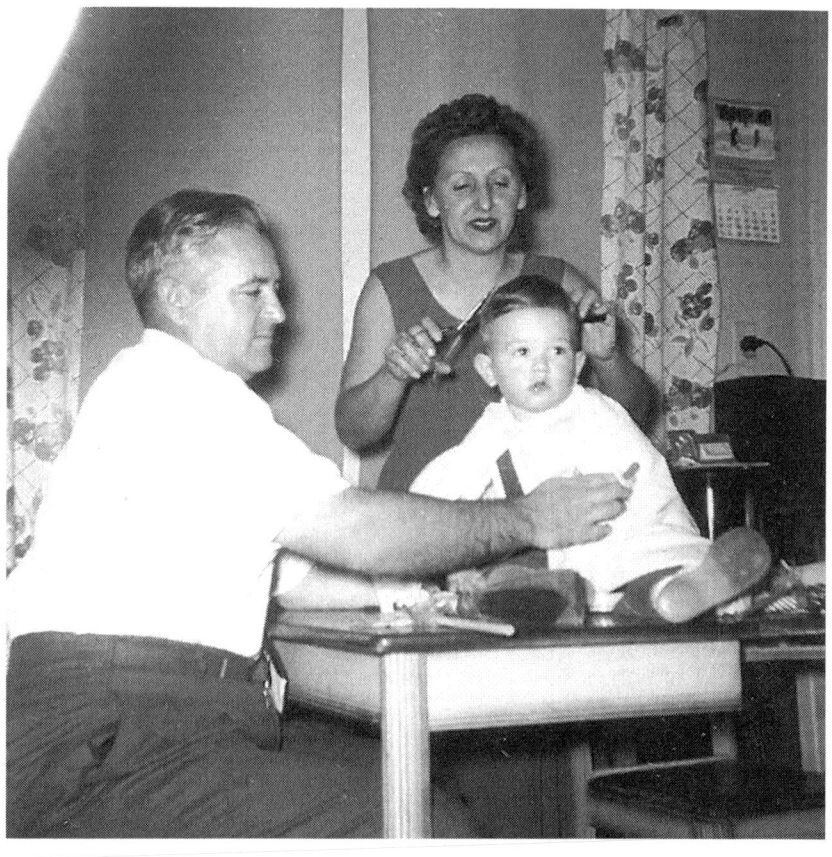

Bob and sister Rose giving the author his first haircut.

# CHAPTER 11
## EPILOG: NOW FOR THE REST OF THE STORIES

When writing a biography of someone who is your father and whom you spent your entire life with (and who lived to be 96), one has hundreds of stories to tell about that person. In writing this book I tried to weave in as many of these Bob stories into the appropriate chapters and places as possible. Many stories didn't fit into the stories told in the chapters that needed to be told to tell the life story of Bob Babbish in its entirety. I will tell these remaining stories, some I witnessed while others I heard of, here in this chapter in no real order of them happening as, otherwise, they will never be told. I am sure that after this book is published I will think of more but these will have to do for now.

<u>Famous Golfers Bob Knew</u>

Bob knew of Walter Hagen, Senior, but only met him once. The time he met *The Haig* was in Chicago in an unrecalled year, probably the late 1930's. They were both playing in a tournament there. Bob ran into him there at the club grill. They ended up spending the entire day talking, as the tournament was rained-out. Walter knew of Bob and of course Bob knew all about Walter. He said they had a great time talking. As you know, Bob later played Walter Junior and beat him in his last college golf game.

Bob once told me another Hagen story. Hagen had a Detroit connection. For a time he was the professional at Tam O'Shanter Country Club in West Bloomfield. While he was there he lived downtown at The Detroit Athletic Club in one of the rooms for members they had upstairs. No one recalls how he ended up staying there but after a number of months the Club sent the manager up there to present Walter his bill for room and board. Turns out he had never paid them a dime and the Club was getting a bit worried.

After knocking politely for what seemed forever, Walter answered the door. The manager hemmed and hawed and beat around the bush some but finally presented the bill to the famous golfer. Walter looked at it and gave it back saying that the Club should be paying him to stay there not the other way around and shut the door in his face.

Bob said that as a result of Walter's response, which made the rounds rather quickly, all the members chipped in and paid Walter's bills for the rest of his stay, which lasted over a year.

Bob knew all the great professional golfers from that era. It was like a social club and a small one at that and they all knew and liked each other. He was there when Ben Hogan declared Oakland Hills "The Monster" during the 1951 U.S. Open. He loved Sam Snead but said he was the cheapest person he had ever met, a description repeated by many others. Byron Nelson was also a friend. Chick Harbert was one of his favorites and he liked to tell the story of how Chick became professional by accident as related earlier. He thought that was so funny. He knew all the Michigan professionals like Horton Smith and Walter Burkemo and Al Watrous. He had also met Francis Ouimet and Bobby Jones, the great amateur golfers from the generation before Bob.

Many of the newspaper articles played up a perpetual feud between the great Michigan amateur golfers that were

Bob's peers. If there was an animosity it was because they all hated to lose. However, they all equally and sincerely cheered each other's victories because they were all friends and colleagues in the rough and tumble world of golf back then. The Glenn Johnson feud: Bob purchased all his insurance from Glenn for many years, starting when they were competing in all those tournaments in the 1950's. Ben Smith and Bob were roommates before Bob married in 1951 and remained great friends until Ben died a few years before Bob did, keeping in touch the whole time. Bob regularly consulted with Chuck Kocsis for tips on improving his golf game and even used some of Chuck's homemade clubs to test them out for him. They were all best friends over the years and golf brought them together.

The golfing world was a pretty tight circle and when a fellow golfer, amateur or professional, was in a bind all the others did their best to help him out. Sol Eisenberg did that by hiring Bob back to his steel company in the 1970's. Walter Burkemo, when he was the pro at Detroit Golf Club in the 1970's, often hired professional golfers that were down and out on their luck as assistant professionals until they could get their feet back on the ground. One I particularly remember and benefited from was Jimmy Thompson. Jimmy was a bit older that Bob and had the reputation in his youth as being the longest distance driver of all the golfers.

When Jimmy showed up as an assistant pro at the Club, Bob, in order to support his old friend, immediately offered me up for his first lesson. I remember hitting a bucket of balls on the range and not one word about my swing from Jimmy, who was busy talking to Bob about old times behind me, the two of them being a bit loud for my concentration. When I had finished my bucket of balls Jimmy came over, told me to take a swing and hold it, and adjusted my ending follow-through swing position. He said to hit another bucket and try to end each swing in that position. This I did and wow, what an improvement. Each ball was hit straight and true and far. I kept that follow-through until this day and when I ever got a compliment for my golf swing it is that I have a great follow-through thanks to an old pro down on his luck that was given a break by some friends.

## Caddying for Bob

When I was a teenager, Bob really wanted me to follow his path in golfing. He knew what it did for him and figured it could do the same for me (I was a difficult kid and he may have figured it was my only hope). He attempted this by having me follow his introduction to golf: caddying. At first he got me a job caddying at Bloomfield Hills Country Club near where we lived. The caddy superintendant there, George Uzulac, was an old friend of Bob's and Bob knew that George would take care of his son in the often cutthroat world of modern-day caddies. I wasn't too hot on caddying but one Saturday morning the home phone rang and it was for me. George was calling asking me why I wasn't at the club yet, that he had a loop for me. Well that embarrassed me to get there to report for work. When I showed up he pointed to a gold-colored golf bag and said that was my bag to carry for my first loop.

Now George knew that I knew a bit about the game as I played some and so I didn't need to be trained as a caddy. I had no idea of how the Bloomfield Hills' course was laid out but he said that didn't matter for this first loop as the golfer did. I carried the bag to the first tee waiting for my member golfer. Soon a tall, flashy-looking guy with silver hair showed up, sees me with his bag and comes over and introduced himself. His name was John Z. DeLorean. I will never forget that he was wearing gold-colored golf shoes that matched his bag.

At that time DeLorean was a Vice President at General Motors Corporation in charge of the Pontiac Division, which he was shaking up. He later quit, wrote a critical book about GM and Detroit, started up DeLorean Motors, and then went to jail. But back then he was just another auto executive who, as many of them did, belonged to the prestigious (and playable) Bloomfield Hills Country Club. (As an aside, the second person I caddied for there was Tony Delorenzo who was the Vice President of Public Relations at GM. George the caddy superintendant had a lot of faith in me to give me such big name executives to caddy for.)

Well, caddying at Bloomfield Hills didn't work out because of my lack of interest so Bob took a different approach. Why should he be paying a caddy that he didn't know to carry his bags at Detroit Golf Club (carts were not always used by golfers back then, usually just by older ones who had trouble walking the course) when Bob had a son that could. So the next thing I know my forced appreciation of the game that my father loved took the form of waking up early every Saturday and Sunday a number of summers and driving the half-hour drive to DGC to caddy for the old man. Granted, he paid me the going rate plus a tip (if I deserved it). The caddy superintendant was OK with it. The sweetener was that he would buy me lunch in the Men's Grill afterwards and we would play golf together in the afternoon. As I said, Bob was an educated man. It not only gave me the golf experience but also gave him the excuse to play 36 holes on Saturday and Sunday as he was with his son the whole time, something that his wife had a hard time protesting about.

This caddying for Bob lasted throughout high school. We had a lot of fun together and Bob was a great teacher, both directly with instructions and indirectly through watching. I also met many great people including a lot of important local celebrities, doctors, lawyers and judges whom were either playing with Bob in the morning or who I played with in the afternoon games. I also was introduced to the golf club life as both a worker and member's son. My game got better with time but the passion was never there for me and when I went to college I pretty much dropped it. For me it was too time consuming as I had other interests back then. Plus I wasn't salesman material and realized it was an expensive sport that I would have to finance myself instead how Bob did it through his company.

As the one person who probably caddied the most times for Bob (every weekend during the season, all through high school and even before and afterwards a bit), I can tell you that he was the easiest loop a caddy could get.

Rarely did Bob's shots land out of the fairway or off of the green. You never really had to watch where his ball landed or to try to find an errant ball. Even the times he had a bad shot he knew exactly where his ball landed. He always knew what his next club was going to be and would grab it when he gave you the last shot's club back to put in the golf bag. He never, ever asked advice from his caddy as to how to make the next shot; didn't have to.

He never used a huge, heavy golf bag like everyone else did back then: he was once a caddy and knew what it was like carrying a ton of bricks on your shoulder all day long. He never filled his golf bag with unnecessary stuff like so many players did, such as an extra pair of golf shoes, umbrella, tons of balls, jacket, etc.

On the course Bob was the professor. With caddies he was always teaching them the game. He did this to not only make them better caddies but to introduce them to golfing. That was the way he was introduced to the game as an eleven-year old in 1926. He always treated the caddies with respect, something that wasn't too common back then. Usually caddies were a non-entity to the members playing golf, just a tool that eventually was replaced with a machine, the golf cart. To Bob, the caddy was someone with great potential, be it as a caddy, a golfer, a businessman, whatever, and there on the golf course they were learning the ways of life and of making a living. He knew that their experiences on the course, usually working their first job, would be carried with them for the rest of their lives. I run into many of Bob's former caddies still.

When I started showing up to caddy for Bob on weekends in the late 1960's the other caddies were not too happy to see me. Gone was the chance of getting the best and easiest loop of the day, plus Bob was a good tipper. I still remember that back then there were a number of "adult" caddies at the Detroit Golf Club, grown men that caddied as their career or supplemented whatever their career was with caddying. Though I do not think they ever caddied for Bob (he liked the younger caddies who he could teach a thing or to about the game and job), I could tell from their stares that they were not too happy with me caddying for him. Plus, Bob often asked me to carry the bag for another player of his foursome, a double-loop, meaning one less caddying job that day for the regular caddies.

A double-loop was a pain physically, having one bag on each shoulder for 18 holes and crisscrossing the course to serve both players. But I really only had to worry about the other player as Bob was pretty much on his own as mentioned above.

Unlike the rest of the caddies, though, I got to enter the clubhouse with him afterwards, shower and eat lunch in the Men's Grill at the Club. That made it all worth caddying for Bob instead of working at a golf course as a caddy closer to my house in the suburbs where you might not even get a loop, least of all eat.

Bob was, as I mentioned, an educated man. This whole thing about me caddying for him wasn't entirely a convenience or a fatherly thing to do. It was his way of introducing me to the game he loved as well as a job. Plus he was able to introduce me to a lot of influential people that belonged to the Club and by working for them as a caddy they were getting to know my work ethic. Once again Bob using this game of golf as something much greater than just a game but a way of life and, though we didn't call it as such back then, for "networking."

Part of this education was about the game of golf and how it was played, not only by watching him play but by a constant stream of instructions from Bob as to how he was going to play that shot, what he was thinking of, the obstacles, the distance to the green (no distance markers back then), etc. He was teaching me to play and I wasn't even swinging a club!

Another part of the education Bob was giving me was that I saw his and the other golfers' attitudes and demeanors, in good times and bad, and learned about the ways to handle golf's and life's situations. Golf is a microcosm of life and one's personality comes through loud and clear during playing this game that you can never control or win. And, as Bob used to tell me, what better way to get to know someone than spend three our four hours with them playing a sport you both loved on a beautiful day outside? Implied but unsaid was what better way to sell a customer steel or whatever you were selling than making the golf course the office where the transaction was being worked out. The South Course at Detroit Golf Club was Bob's office as well as his playground.

## Bob's Other Sports

Bob did like other sports, especially hockey and baseball since he played both in high school. This took the form later in his life of attending Detroit Red Wing hockey and Detroit Tiger baseball games as a spectator.

At one time Bob had front row season tickets for the Red Wings when they played at the old Olympia Stadium (which they did until 1980). Bob no longer had these seats when I was around but he often was able to get tickets to Red Wing games and take me to them. Usually they were in a business suite that a neighbor had with his company. They hung from the bottom front of the upper deck at Olympia Stadium and were rather rough but were isolated from the crowds, were really close to the ice, and had an open bar so I could drink as much pop and eat as many nuts as I wanted without having to buy them.

As mentioned, my middle-name-sake Charlie Escoe provided Bob with plenty of Tiger baseball game tickets at the old Tiger Stadium. We never knew where we would be sitting from game to game but they were always box seats in a good location.

## Bob The Handyman

Anyone who knew Bob would laugh at this title as a handyman Bob was not. When he moved into the new house on Darcy Drive in 1960, though, he did make an attempt to be one. It failed and he later said, "That's why I had a son."

Bob had quite a large lawn to maintain on Darcy. Prior to that he had a postage stamp-sized lawn on Muirland Street that he could handle with a manual push-mower like everyone had in the city back then. For Darcy, Bob needed a lawn tractor. These were not very common back then as the suburbs and large lawns were just being created. He went to the only lawn equipment store around, Manus Power Mowers on Woodward Avenue in Royal Oak, and purchased one.

I was thrilled with this idea and was so excited about Bob getting one. Now we were really living in the country, I thought. All country dwellers needed a tractor. I was a bit disappointed as to how small it was when it arrived. I guess I was expecting a full-sized Ford tractor like you'd see on all the farms. But, what the heck, it was self-propelled and you sat on it. It was a tractor.

I remember watching with pride Bob starting it up the first time, getting on it and actually cutting the grass. I couldn't wait until I was old enough to do this. Cutting the grass with it seemed like the greatest thing a kid could do. As I was watching Bob cut the lawn that first time I realized that the yard sloped a bit into a drainage ditch along the front of the yard next to the street. Each house there had a culvert pipe under their driveway and this dip in the lawn was for those big rains when the water ran off and filled up these ditches in the front lawns instead of flooding the street. Not knowing the proper way to operate the lawn tractor on a hill, Bob promptly flipped it over on himself within the first minutes of using it. I was shocked, not so much out of worry for Bob's safety, as he seemed OK, but about maybe breaking my beloved new lawn tractor. Afterwards, Bob flipped it back upright and carefully drove it into the garage, not saying a word and not finishing the lawn.

The next day the Manus Power Mowers delivery truck showed up again and they loaded the lawn tractor into it and took it away. Bob had returned it, saying it was too dangerous to use. Manus dropped off a small walk-behind Toro gas-powered mower to replace the lawn tractor. I knew even then that if Bob had gone up and down that slight slope in the front yard instead of riding along the slope like he did he would have been not tipped it over. But the lawn tractor was gone before I could explain and protest.

Another related tractor story is from that first winter on Darcy Drive as Bob had to worry about shoveling a very large circular driveway. There were no snowplowing services back then: You did it by yourself. One day he told me that he was going to purchase a "snow plow" to shovel the snow.

Well, I must have been still lamenting the loss of the lawn tractor as that sounded to me like Bob was going to buy another tractor, this one with a snow blade to plow the snow off the driveway. That made perfect sense as the circular driveway we had was huge and there wasn't any way you could hand-shovel it. Soon the big day came that Bob was bringing home the snow plow. I waited anxiously for him to come home from work with it. When he did he was just driving his usual Buick. No trailer containing a tractor or anything. No Manus delivery truck following him. I asked him where was the snowplow? "In the trunk," he said. What? How could that be?

Bob opened up the trunk and pulled out a snow "shovel," not a snow plow. And it was really a coal shovel, very small for shoveling snow. Boy was I disappointed. I pointed out to him it was a bit small and he replied, "easier for you to handle." I still have that "snow plow" and laugh every time I use it, which is often, since when there is a heavy snow I use that to shovel instead of the wider shovels that get too heavy with snow.

I only remember Bob washing the windows on the house on Darcy twice. The first time he was washing the outside of the large "picture" window in the font of the house and it cracked. It must have been defective but I thought that was bad luck.

The second time was when Bob was out back washing the outside of the upstairs windows. He had to borrow an extension ladder from Mr. Jung down the street to do this and Bob was up high on the ladder and I was holding it on the ground for support. I was looking up at Bob washing the second floor windows and suddenly he looked like he was going to fall off the ladder. Then he recovered and yelled down to me, "What the heck was that? It almost knocked me off the ladder!" I hadn't noticed anything and said that I didn't know what he was talking about.

Bob quickly got off that ladder and abandoned the window washing for that day and forever. I was suspicious until we read in the newspaper the next morning that there was a rare, slight earthquake in the area the prior day, the first one in fifty years. You guessed it, Bob was at the top of an extension ladder the moment the earthquake occurred. Just Bob's handyman luck. I took over this chore too after that. Bob would pay me $1 an hour to do "his" chores around the house. They were taking away from his playing golf anyway and "that's why he had a son."

The only tools Bob ever owned were a small hammer, pliers and needle nose pliers and he never used them. I have all three and still use them all the time. This is probably the reason that Bob never was interested in building his own golf clubs like many other golfers were.

## Dreaming Golf

After a rough day at work (i.e., on the golf course), Bob would come home and often fall asleep on a hammock we had on the back porch on Darcy Drive. Sure, he started off saying that he was going to read the paper and relax but before too long you could hear the snoring and Bob was out like a light. Sometimes if it was after dinner the only thing that would wake him up and drive him back into the house were the mosquitoes that came out after dark.

Bob equated lying in a hammock with the good life. Maybe it was an old farm thing. The only times I ever saw Bob read a book were in that hammock but they always put him to sleep. They were also always books about golf.

I tell this story as one time Mom asked me to wake up Bob for dinner. I went to do so and couldn't without really shaking him awake. That hammock was really swinging away. When Bob finally woke up and realized it was me and time for dinner he said, "Oh, Byron, I was just putting for eagle and you woke me up. Now I won't know if I made it."

I thought that was so funny. What a great sense of humor Bob had to come up with this line even when he was still drowsy.

Well, similar lines about golfing in his dreams came up whenever I woke him up over the years, even much later in life. I always figured it was our little joke. One day when he was old I asked him about this.

Bob said it was no joke, he was dreaming about golf. That he always dreamt about playing golf. Didn't everyone? I then realized exactly what golf meant to Bob. I really understood it later in my life when I developed an interest in trains. Guess what I dream about every night?

## Bob's Memory

Bob had a remarkable memory. Sometimes I thought he remembered everything that ever happened to him his entire life. Anytime I mentioned an event from our family he remembered it, better than I did. This lasted until his final stroke two weeks before he died.

This memory was very acute when it came to golf. Bob seemed like he could remember every round of golf he ever played, routine or tournament, every hole on every course, every shot on every round of golf, who he played with and his score. It was unbelievable. I couldn't relate to this until later in my life with my railroad interest. I can remember just about every train I ever saw, where it was, etc. I guess that just comes with the hobby you love. Or I got Bob's memory gene.

## Golf Equipment

As Bob started playing golf in 1926 with used equipment, we presume he started with wood-shafted clubs even though steel shafts were coming in use by then. Bob had a wood-shafted putter among his many clubs over the years though I do not recall him using it but once when he was really having troubles on the green and was trying all his putters out to correct it. He did win the 1938 Western Amateur with one, maybe the same putter.

Bob was a strong guy and always had really stiff-shafted clubs. I could never use them when I was a kid as I was tall and lanky and just sliced all my shots with them. I did get one set of clubs from Bob when I was a bit older and stronger and still have them.

Back when he was really a competitor, a friend of his who worked for a local golf club company, Gorman Golf, would custom-build him clubs. Stan Sabbit was a friend of Bob's from the old neighborhood and was always experimenting with different club designs and Bob was the unpaid showcase of Gorman clubs in action. I remember us often visiting Stan at Gorman Golf, located in Southfield, Michigan at 12 Mile Road and Telegraph Roads, during the winter. Bob would stop to say hello and we would hit some balls in their inside net to stay in shape. First inside golf range I had ever seen.

Bob never had a completely matched set of clubs in his bag when I was caddying for him. His driver was always a unique one and usually his other woods were made by some company other than the driver or the irons. His sand wedge was usually a very old one and different than the other irons. He often carried a Number 1 iron and I remember him using it a lot. I remember he was using a "jigger" club to chip with for a while, one of his from his younger days that he kept. I used it for a while when chipping onto the greens. Nice club. He usually used a Titleist blade putter from the 1960's and one of those odd Ping putters for awhile. But when the putting went bad he would go to the golf closet and start trying out all his old putters.

His first concession to getting older was removing his Number 1 iron from the bag and using a six or eight wood instead. He hated doing so but admitted it really helped his game when his distance was diminishing.

Bob never wore a golf glove and rarely a hat when playing. He always used a very tall tee and whenever he found any for sale would buy a ton of them as they were hard to find. He needed them because of his "jump" on his drives.

Bob loved to play in short pants and be comfortable in the hot weather. He didn't care what others thought. He had no style for clothing. He always wore an Izod golf shirt, the ones with the alligator on them. Back then those shirts could only be purchased at a golf pro shop. He also wore Izod golf socks, the ones with the two stripes at the top. He had a large assortment of golf shoes, the old kind with the spikes, but I do not recall him ever buying any; it seemed that someone was always giving Bob golf shoes.

## Playing Golf with Bob

I played golf with Bob almost every weekend afternoon during the season for those years I caddied for him. That was the deal: caddy for Bob in the morning and play with him in the afternoon. Not a bad situation for a high school kid.

Those golf lessons in the morning while caddying (either the explicit ones or implicit ones) were put to the test in the afternoon when I was hitting the ball. I would usually carry Bob's bag as well as mine in the afternoon. Almost every shot of mine received a comment from Bob, from one extreme, "That's the way to stroke it," to the other, "You can hit it better than that, drop another ball and hit it again." Needless to say, if I shot a 90 for that round I probably hit closer to 180 balls playing with Bob!

Bob also taught me the formal rules of golf as well as golf etiquette. He was always a fast player and was thinking ahead a couple of shots and liked to keep the pace moving instead of bogging down. He was never afraid of asking a slower foursome in front of him if he could "play through" them and when they saw it was Bob they always would oblige. This is one reason he liked to play early in the morning on weekends; to be the first foursome off so no one was playing in front of him to slow down his pace. He usually finished eighteen holes of golf in three hours or maybe less if he was on DGC's South Course. This gave him an earlier start in the afternoon to play another round and still get home to take a nap in the hammock on the patio before dinner.

As mentioned, everyone wanted to play with Bob. During the week this mostly meant customers. What better way to "work" than to do so playing golf? On weekends in the mornings he had his usual group of friends that were like-minded as he was about playing quickly with no-nonsense. These include the likes of Dick Krajenke, John Scott, Bud Linderman, Dr. Jaffar and other early birds who were all decent golfers. In the afternoons on weekends when I was playing the foursomes became a bit more strategic for my benefit. Remember, golf opened up the business world to Bob and he was hoping it would do the same for me. If one of his friends had a son or daughter who played golf, like Krajenke's or Andre's or Gargaro's, we often had a foursome consisting of two fathers and two children.

Most of the time, though, Bob prearranged an afternoon game with one or two important members of the Club. These were often doctors, lawyers, judges, successful businessmen, celebrities and sometimes golf pros. There was scheme to this madness and maybe it worked as eventually as I did end up becoming a lawyer. I played with J.P. McArthy, the famous longtime WJR morning radio host, Joe Muer and Hector Sousi, the famous Detroit restaurant owners, William Henry Gallagher, the lawyer who defeated Henry Ford in court (I didn't know this until later in life), famous doctors like Donald Jaffar and the Porretta brothers, golf professionals and great amateurs like Bobby Inman, Glenn Johnson and Ben Smith, car dealership owners like Dick Krajenke and Zip Ellis and many many others. Golf really opened up my world like it did Bob's, only I didn't have the talent for it like he did.

My two most memorable moments playing golf with Bob were when we won the DGC Father and Son Championship and when I broke 80 for a round.

As to the Father and Son Championship at the Detroit Golf Club, we had played in this tournament for years during high school and college, always coming up short because of my playing. Then in 1975 we finally won it. I do not remember all the details of that victory other than my handicap and a good round of playing clinched it for us. I still have the prize we received for it sitting on my kitchen windowsill: an engraved pewter mug. This was the only golf event I ever won, other than winning the farcical Hamtramck Open one Sunday morning.

As to breaking 80, Bob and I were playing one Sunday afternoon on DGC's South Course (par 68) and I was doing rather well. Bob was afraid to say anything but all I needed coming off of the Number 16 hole was a par for the last two holes, Number 17 being a short par 3 and Number 18 being a medium-length par 4, to card a 79.

I had a great seven-iron on 17 onto the green and got down with two-putts for a par. Now all I needed was a par on 18. This was the time I usually would have collapsed. Probably because I figured I would collapse I nonchalantly hit my drive on 18 and it was a good one, right down the center of the fairway. My next shot was a Number 4 iron and it too was hit well, landing on the green about 20 feet from the cup. Bob wasn't saying anything but I usually was a pretty good putter and getting down in two from where I was should be easy and result in a 79. I went up and stroked the putt and it went into the hole for a birdie! Not only did I break 80 but did so by two strokes with a 78. I quit golfing after that, figuring I had reached my peak.

## Holes-In-One

Bob had thirteen holes-in-one during his golfing career, the last one being when he was 89 years old! Actually, for some reason most of Bob's holes-in-one happened when he was considered a senior golfer.

I remember this because when I was caddying and playing with him during high school there used to be a hole-in-one board in the clubhouse at Detroit Golf Club. I remember it having the names of all the golfers at the Club who had made a hole-in-one and at what hole and what year. During that time only one hole-in-one appeared next to Bob's name. Other members, including many "duffers," had a lot more holes-in-one next to their names. I found this a bit baffling and even embarrassing. What, The Great Babbish with only one ace?

I once asked Bob about this deficiency in his golf record. He told me that it was a good thing, that it was too expensive to have a hole-in-one. Too expensive? Turns out that anytime someone got a hole-in-one at the Club, when he came into the clubhouse afterwards (and by that time everyone knew it had happened and were calling all their friends who were rushing to get to the Club before the ace finished his round) he had to buy drinks for everyone. He said that a hole-in-one, even one during the week when not many members were there, could cost you over a hundred dollars for the bar tab.

So this did not answer the question but at least it didn't bother Bob like it bothered me. At some point the Club instituted a hole-in-one insurance policy where at the beginning of the year everyone put up $20 and the fund was used to buy drinks for anyone who got a hole-in-one.

## Important Detroit Golf Club Members

John Cardinal Dearden was the archbishop of Detroit from 1958 to 1980. I never heard Bob say anything nice about Cardinal Dearden as he thought the Cardinal was way too liberal. He was and he was not only an important person in Detroit but also in Rome. So why am I talking about Cardinal Dearden here in a book about Bob Babbish? Back then Detroit Golf Club gave an honorary membership to the Archbishop of Detroit. I think this was not only a courtesy to the position but it also enhanced the standing of the membership of the club. Plus back then the Archbishop lived in a house in the Palmer Woods neighborhood, which was located just across 7 Mile Road from DGC, and so was a neighbor.

Anyway, regardless of what Bob thought about Cardinal Dearden's political persuasion, he was a fellow member of his club and so they shared an interest in golf. And like most golfers, the Cardinal wanted to play golf with Bob to hopefully pick up a few pointers to improve his game (Bob said that His Eminence was not a very good golfer). So a few times a year Cardinal Dearden played golf with Bob. The only problem was that this golf thing and being a member of a golf club didn't exactly go along with Dearden's liberal social justice bent and His Eminence knew it. Such it is with golf: the passion for it overcomes the intellect against it. So these golf games with Bob usually had to be kept somewhat a secret if possible.

Bob never told me about them until after Cardinal Dearden's death in 1981, the secret was so important. Sort of like a reverse confession with Bob the absolver. The games were always played during the week, usually in the late afternoon, just Bob and the Cardinal as a two-some.

I remember Bob telling me the story about some large

dinner event at DGC that he attended. He was sitting at a table with friends including our neighbor at the time, D'Arcy O'Neil. The Cardinal was at the event too and was sitting at a table on the other side of the banquet room.

At some point the Cardinal was trying to get Bob's attention from across the room. D'Arcy picked up on this and brought it to Bob's attention. Bob excused himself and went to see what His Eminence wanted. After chatting with the Cardinal for a bit, kneeling next to him, Bob came back to his table and said nothing about it. D'Arcy couldn't contain his curiosity and flat out asked Bob what the Cardinal wanted. Bob replied, "To hear my confession." D'Arcy and the others at the table didn't know if this was a good thing or a bad thing but it did explain his kneeling. What could Bob have done to warrant the Cardinal demanding him to come to him for confession? Truth was that Cardinal Dearden only wanted to collar Bob to set up a golf game that week, which they played, quietly, late one afternoon.

K. T. Keller was President of Chrysler Corporation from 1935 to 1950 and then its Chairman until 1956. Under his leadership Chrysler became the second largest automotive company. Chrysler Corporation's headquarters were located in Highland Park, another city that the City of Detroit expanded past but never did absorb, a city within a city, that was located just a couple miles from Detroit Golf Club.

K. T. Keller was a member of Detroit Golf Club. I do not know if this was another free membership or if he or Chrysler paid for it, but either way it added prestige to the Club. He was a very important person in Detroit at the time but at the Club was just another member, equal in rank and status as every other member.

Bob used to say that K. T. Keller ate lunch at the Club

every workday. This is logical as he did work just down the street from the Club and business life was a lot different back then. The Detroit District Golf Association Championship trophy was named after him. One of the waiters in the Men's Grill, Chris, once told me the story of what a regular guy K. T. was.

He said that one of the other waiters, a long-time employee who was still there when I was playing, was K. T.'s favorite waiter. That K.T. always insisted that he serve his table. The funny part of the story is that no one else really liked this waiter but K. T. One reason being that his waiter skills were a bit lacking. For instance, when he delivered the water or drinks, he held the glass with his thumb inside of it in the drink, a mortal sin for a waiter. But K. T. either never noticed or didn't mind.

When Lee Iacocca became Chairman of Chrysler in 1979, Bob, who didn't personally know Lee but did know a lot of Chrysler executives who did know him, suggested that DGC give Lee an honorary membership. The Club agreed and Bob got the word out to Lee through his friend and fellow member Cecil Chauvin, who worked at Chrysler. But Lee didn't take them up on it. By then it wasn't politically correct for a chairman of a struggling company to be found spending time at a country club and I think he already belonged to Bloomfield Hills Golf Club closer to his house.

Another important person that DGC offered an honorary membership too was Coleman A. Young, the first African-American mayor of Detroit. This was seen as an important step for DGC as it was being criticized for not having many (if any) minorities as members back in 1974 when Mayor Young was elected. Bob was 100% behind this idea. His Honor accepted the membership but I don't recall him ever showing up at the Club. This started the tradition of DGC giving each of the subsequent mayors of Detroit an honorary membership.

## 1988 Western Amateur Championship

In 1988 Bob was invited by the Western Golf Association to play in a ceremonial round of golf at the beginning of that year's Western Amateur Tournament to celebrate the 50th anniversary of him winning it in 1938. It was being held in Benton Harbor, Michigan at Point O' Woods Golf and Country Club, its home course for a number of years back then. They also invited two other past Michigan contestants who never won it but who were once runners-up, Chuck Kocsis and Tommy Sheehan, to play with Bob, both being good friends of him. Bob flew up from Florida for it and I took the day off of work and drove him to Benton Harbor, located on the west side of Michigan.

It was the first time I met either Chuck or Tommy but the friendship between the three of them was very apparent. They played 18 holes immediately before the contestants played with one of the tournament officials acting as their caddy and guide. There were a lot of newspaper reporters there for the event and they all interviewed Bob and his friends too. I brought along my new, bulky videocassette recorder and taped most of the golf round, concentrating on Bob. I was able to catch their conversations that included reminiscing about old times and tournaments and giving each other golfing tips, something that never ends and is always appreciated (Bob did not play well that day and was constantly consulting with Chuck and Tommy for advice. "You are never too old to learn," Bob used to say.)

I still have the videotape and played it before I started

writing this book. It is a classic. Three old golf heroes playing a leisurely game of golf in the twilight of their careers. Having a great time and not caring about their scores for a change but still trying to play well so as not to embarrass themselves. Tommy Sheehan died just a year or two later. Chuck Kocsis lived many more years but not as long as Bob who outlived them all. I imagine they are all still playing golf together in heaven with all the rest of the old time golfers they grew up playing with, still giving and taking tips on their swing and putting to each other.

A golfer like Bob never stopped being a golfer. It was the focus of his life. Everything revolved around golf. God, family, golf, and not necessarily in that order. What is it about this sport that causes this more so than any other? You can never perfect it. It is always beating you. You basically play against the course and yourself, as it is not a team sport by nature. Maybe all these things are what make this game so special and maybe what makes golfers like The Great Babbish so special as human beings. For Bob, golf was truly a madness, something that he could not tame on the course, though he tamed it better than most everyone else. Golf madness. But instead of conquering him like a madness usually does to the human, Bob used it make him a better person and give him more opportunities in life.

Bob's golf madness was the American Dream for him. And it all started at work one day when he was eleven years old, supporting his family by carrying a bag of golf clubs for some golfer in 1926 at Orchard Lake Country Club. I often wonder who was that first golfer on that first loop Bob had and if he ever knew what came out of that day. It was the greatest tip Bob ever received.

# List of Known Golfing Events of Bob Babbish

| 1930 | Detroit District Golf Association (DDGA) Caddy Championship; led Orchard Lake Country Club caddies to a team victory |
|------|---|
| 1931 | DDGA Caddy Championship at Meadowbrook Country Club; led Detroit Golf Club caddies to team victory and won the individual championship |
| 1932 | 12th Annual Detroit City Golf League tournament; led Pershing High School to a victory |
| 1933 | Won the Public Links Tournament at Bob 'O Links Golf Club |
| 1934 | Won the Michigan Golf Association Open Amateur at Bonnie Brook Golf Club defeating Larry Olpalka and Bill Fenwick |
| | Played in the National Public Links Tournament held at Pittsburgh, PA. Qualified in number one position for Michigan's team. It was Bob's first national tournament and he made it to the third round |
| | Runner-up in Michigan Amateur |
| | Joined Beverly Hills Country Club |
| 1935 | Won Michigan Amateur at Belvedere Country Club in Charlevoix beating Ed Novak |
| | Reached the DDGA District Championship semifinals |
| | Joined Brooklands Golf and Country Club |
| 1936 | Runner-up in Michigan Amateur |
| | Reached DDGA District Championship semifinals at Essexville |
| 1937 | Won Michigan Open Amateur at Rammler Golf Club, Sterling Heights, Michigan, beating Drew Engleston in playoff |
| | Played in National Amateur Championship in Portland, Oregon. Lost in first round 4 to 3 to John Fisher |
| | Runner-up Michigan Amateur |
| | Runner-up Michigan Open |
| | Reached DDGA District Championship semifinals |
| 1938 | Won Western Amateur at South Bend, Indiana |

| | |
|---|---|
| | Qualified for and played in the U. S. Open at Cherry Hills Golf Club in Denver, Colorado; finished 55th place, fifth low amateur, won by Ralph Guldahl |
| | Semifinalist at the National Collegiate Championship held in Louisville, Kentucky, loosing to John P. Burke of Georgetown University shooting a 79 and 75 |
| | Contender for position on 1940 Walker Cup Team but the tournament was canceled that year due to World War II |
| 1939 | Qualified for and played in the U.S. Open at Philadelphia Country Club, Gladwyne, Pennsylvania, won by Byron Nelson |
| | Runner-up Michigan Open at Western Golf Club to Marvin Stahl by 1 stroke |
| 1940 | Qualified for and played in the U.S. Open at Canterbury Golf Club, Beachwood, Ohio; finished in 52nd place, his best for a U.S. Open, won by Lawson Little |
| | Won DDGA Championship at Meadowbrook beating Christ Burke in 13 holes |
| 1941–1944 | War Years |
| 1945 | Played in Michigan Open |
| 1946 | Qualified for and played in the U.S. Open at Canterbury Country Club, Beachwood, Ohio, won by Lloyd Mangrum |
| | Played in U.S. Amateur Championship at Baltusrol, New Jersey |
| | Ranked as #10 of Michigan Golfers in DDGA's first Annual Honor Roll |
| | Joined Red Run Golf Club |
| 1947 | Qualified for U.S. Amateur at Riveria Country Club, Palisades, California but did not play in it |
| | DDGA Honor Roll #3 |
| 1948 | Qualified for and played in the U.S. Open at St. Louis Country Club, Ladue, Missouri, won by Ben Hogan |
| | DDGA Honor Roll #1 |
| 1949 | DDGA Honor Roll #2 |
| | Won Franklin Country Club Invitational, Franklin, Michigan |
| | Won Blythefield Country Club Invitational, Grand Rapids |

| | |
|---|---|
| 1950 | Won DDGA District Championship 3 to 2 over Dick Whiting at Lochmoor Country Club |
| | Played in Michigan Amateur at Gull Lake Country Club, Kalamazoo; lost to Nap Chinick in second round |
| | Motor City Open low amateur at Red Run Golf Club in Royal Oak beating Ben Hogan by 1 stroke; Lloyd Mangrum was the winner |
| | Played in National Amateur in Minneapolis, qualifying with a 141 at Country Club of Detroit |
| | DDGA Honor Roll #5 |
| 1951 | DDGA Honor Roll #1 |
| | Qualified for and played in the U.S. Open at Oakland Hills Country Club in Bloomfield Hills with a 72/70 142. Ben Hogan won and Bob was the leading amateur after the first round |
| | Joined Detroit Golf Club |
| 1952 | Runner-up in DDGA District Championship loosing to Dick Whiting but won Medalist honors with a 70 |
| | Won Bill Waite Memorial Tournament (Fred Waring sponsored) at Shawnee Inn and Golf Resort in Pennsylvania |
| 1953 | Won DDGA District Championship by beating Ray Iceberg 1 up in three playoff holes |
| | Qualified or and played in the U.S. Open at Oakmont Golf Club in Oakmont, Pennsylvania. Ben Hogan won and Bob's results are not recalled |
| | Low Amateur at Michigan Open |
| | Won Blythefield Country Club Invitational in Grand Rapids |
| | Won Red Run Golf Club Invitational |
| | Won Orchard Lake Country Club Best Ball Invitational |
| 1954 | Won DDGA District Championship for fourth and final time |
| | Qualified (as medalist) and played in National Amateur at Country Club of Detroit, going to the third round, won by Arnold Palmer |
| | DDGA Honor Roll #2 |
| | Won Detroit Golf Club Club Championship for first time |
| | Played in Bing Crosby National Pro-Am at Pebble Beach |
| | Won Pine Lake Country Club Invitational in West Bloomfield |
| | Won Red Run Golf Club Invitational |

| | |
|---|---|
| 1955 | Semifinalist in Michigan Amateur at Jackson Country Club, Jackson, Michigan loosing to Glenn Johnson |
| | Runner-up in DDGA District Championship, losing to Glenn Johnson |
| | DDGA Honor Roll #2 |
| | Reached semifinals of Michigan Open, defeated by Glenn Johnson |
| | Won inaugural Dearborn Country Club Invitational with George Hain by 12 strokes in medal play |
| 1956 | Michigan Medal Play champion at Detroit Golf Club |
| | Won Dearborn Country Club Invitations with George Hain |
| | Low medalist at American-Italian Golf Association Invitational at Bridgeview Golf Club in Columbus, Ohio with a 68 |
| | Won Grosse Isle Country Club Invitational |
| 1957 | Michigan Medal Play champion at Detroit Golf Club winning by 12 strokes and playing even par |
| | Low qualifier for U.S. Amateur Golf Championship at Brookline, Massachusetts qualifying for the seventh time |
| | Qualified for the U.S. Open for the eighth time at Oakmont Country Club in Pennsylvania but had to withdraw beforehand |
| | Runner-up in Black River Country Club Invitational in Port Huron, Michigan with partner Bud Gould |
| | Won Detroit Golf Club Spring Medal Play Tournament |
| 1958 | Played in Bing Crosby National Pro-Am at Pebble Beach |
| 1959 | Played in Bing Crosby National Pro-Am at Pebble Beach |
| 1960 | Competed in Michigan Medal Play championship |
| | Won Detroit Golf Club Club Championship |
| 1962 | Won Detroit Golf Club Club Championship |
| 1963 | Won Pine Lake Country Club Invitational |
| 1973 | Won Detroit Golf Club Senior Club Championship |
| 1974 | Won Detroit Golf Club Senior Club Championship |
| 1975 | Won Detroit Golf Club Senior Club Championship |
| 1979 | Inducted into the Michigan Amateur Sports Hall of Fame |
| 1980 | Won Detroit Golf Club Senior Club Championship |
| | Inducted into the University of Detroit Titan Sports Hall of Fame |

| 1981 | Won Detroit Golf Club Senior Club Championship |
|------|------------------------------------------------|
| 1989 | Inducted into the Michigan Golf Hall of Fame |
| | Won Florida Senior Medal Play Championship |

## Summary of Major Golf Tournaments of Bob Babbish

- Michigan Open-Amateur Champion, 1934 and 1937
- Michigan Amateur Champion, 1935
- Michigan Open Runner-up, 1937
- Western Amateur Champion, 1938
- Semi-Finalist in National Collegiate, 1938
- Detroit District Golf Association Champion 1940, 1950, 1953 and 1954
- Low Amateur and 8th Place Motor City Open 1950
- Michigan Medalist Champion 1956 and 1957
- Qualified for the U. S. Amateur 7 times and played 5 times
- Qualified for the U. S. Open 8 times and played 7 times.

# ABOUT THE AUTHOR

Byron Babbish became the keeper of all Bob Babbish's golf and war articles and photographs when Bob sold his Detroit home and moved to Florida full time in 1984. After the box of Bob's stuff was sitting in the attic for thirty years, he finally took it down and read through it all. Of course this was three years after Bob's death so Bob wasn't around to ask questions about anything or fill in the gaps. But through the saved information came Bob's life story as conveyed in those newspaper articles and photographs. These plus the author's recollection of stories from growing up as Bob's son convinced him that *Golf Madness: The Life Story of Bob Babbish* had to be written. Better late than never. Above is the authoring busy writing Golf Madness on the kitchen table with many of the newspaper clippings out for reference. Elaine Babbish photograph.

Made in the USA
Charleston, SC
07 February 2016